VOLUME FOUR

Nikki Grimes to Suzy Kline

Favorite Children's
AUTHORS *and*
ILLUSTRATORS

E. Russell Primm III, Editor in Chief

PO Box 326, Chanhassen, MN 55317-0326
800/599-READ
http://www.childsworld.com

A Note to Our Readers:

The publication dates listed in each author's or illustrator's selected bibliography represent the date of first publication in the United States.

The editors have listed literary awards that were announced prior to August 2006.

Every effort has been made to contact copyright holders of material included in this reference work. If any errors or omissions have occurred, corrections will be made in future editions.

Photographs: 8—Nikki Grimes; 12, 64, 68, 76, 120—Simon & Schuster; 16—Carlo Ontal / HarperCollins; 20, 36, 104—Scholastic; 24, 52, 56—HarperCollins; 28—Tom Beckley / HarperCollins; 32—Kerlan Collection, University of Minnesota; 40—Random House; 44, 96, 124, 128—Penguin Putnam; 48—Stephen Pingry / Tulsa World / AP Photo; 60—de Grummond Collection, University of Southern Mississippi; 72—Bruce Stotesbury / Farrar, Straus, and Giroux; 80—Library of Congress; 84—Johanna Hurwitz; 88—Photocraft, Ltd. / HarperCollins; 92—Jean K. Aull / Trina Shart Hyman; 108—Gordon Trice; 112—Philip Gould / HarperCollins; 116—Hyperion; 136—Allan Einhorn / HarperCollins; 140—Farrar, Straus, and Giroux; 144—Candlewick Press; 148—Karen Hoyle / Kerlan Collection, University of Minnesota; 152—Suzy Kline.

An Editorial Directions book

Library of Congress Cataloging-in-Publication Data

Favorite children's authors and illustrators / E. Russell Primm III, editor-in-chief. — 2nd ed.
　　v. cm.
　Includes bibliographical references and index.
　Contents: v. 1. Verna Aardema to Ashley Bryan.
　ISBN-13: 978-1-59187-057-9 (v.1 : alk. paper)
　ISBN-10: 1-59187-057-7 (v. 1 : alk. paper)
　ISBN-13: 978-1-59187-058-6 (v. 2 : alk. paper)
　ISBN-10: 1-59187-058-5 (v. 2 : alk. paper)
　ISBN-13: 978-1-59187-059-3 (v. 3 : alk. paper)
　ISBN-10: 1-59187-059-3 (v. 3 : alk. paper)
　ISBN-13: 978-1-59187-060-9 (v. 4 : alk. paper)
　ISBN-10: 1-59187-060-7 (v. 4 : alk. paper)
　ISBN-13: 978-1-59187-061-6 (v. 5 : alk. paper)
　ISBN-10: 1-59187-061-5 (v. 5 : alk. paper)
　ISBN-13: 978-1-59187-062-3 (v. 6 : alk. paper)
　ISBN-10: 1-59187-062-3 (v. 6 : alk. paper)
　ISBN-13: 978-1-59187-063-0 (v. 7 : alk. paper)
　ISBN-10: 1-59187-063-1 (v. 7 : alk. paper)
　ISBN-13: 978-1-59187-064-7 (v. 8 : alk. paper)
　ISBN-10: 1-59187-064-X (v. 8 : alk. paper)
　1. Children's literature—Bio-bibliography—Dictionaries—Juvenile literature. 2. Young adult literature Bio-bibliography—Dictionaries—Juvenile literature. 3. Illustrators—Biography—Dictionaries—Juvenile literature. 4. Children—Books and reading—Dictionaries—Juvenile literature. 5. Young Adults—Books and reading—Dictionaries—Juvenile literature. I. Primm, E. Russell, 1958–
　PN1009.A1F38 2007
　809'.8928203—dc22
　[B]　　　　　　　　　　2006011358

TABLE OF CONTENTS

MAJOR CHILDREN'S AUTHOR AND ILLUSTRATOR LITERARY AWARDS

THE AMERICAN BOOK AWARDS
Awarded from 1980 to 1983 in place of the National Book Award to give national recognition to achievement in several categories of children's literature

THE BOSTON GLOBE–HORN BOOK AWARDS
Established in 1967 by Horn Book *magazine and the* Boston Globe *newspaper to honor the year's best fiction, poetry, nonfiction, and picture books for children*

THE CALDECOTT MEDAL
Established in 1938 and presented by the Association for Library Service to Children division of the American Library Association to illustrators for the most distinguished picture book for children from the preceding year

THE CARNEGIE MEDAL
Established in 1936 and presented by the British Library Association for an outstanding book for children written in English

THE CARTER G. WOODSON BOOK AWARDS
Established in 1974 and presented by the National Council for the Social Studies for the most distinguished social science books appropriate for young readers that depict ethnicity in the United States

THE CORETTA SCOTT KING AWARDS
Established in 1970 in connection with the American Library Association to honor African American authors and illustrators whose books are deemed outstanding, educational, and inspirational

THE HANS CHRISTIAN ANDERSEN MEDAL
Established in 1956 by the International Board on Books for Young People to honor an author or illustrator, living at the time of nomination, whose complete works have made a lasting contribution to children's literature

THE KATE GREENAWAY MEDAL

Established by the Youth Libraries Group of the British Library Association in 1956 to honor illustrators of children's books published in the United Kingdom

THE LAURA INGALLS WILDER AWARD

Established by the Association for Library Service to Children division of the American Library Association in 1954 to honor an author or illustrator whose books, published in the United States, have made a substantial and lasting contribution to children's literature

THE MICHAEL L. PRINTZ AWARD

Established by the Young Adult Library Services division of the American Library Association in 2000 to honor literary excellence in young adult literature (fiction, nonfiction, poetry, or anthology)

THE NATIONAL BOOK AWARDS

Established in 1950 to give national recognition to achievement in fiction, nonfiction, poetry, and young people's literature

THE NEWBERY MEDAL

Established in 1922 and presented by the Association for Library Service to Children division of the American Library Association for the most distinguished contribution to children's literature in the preceding year

THE ORBIS PICTUS AWARD FOR OUTSTANDING NONFICTION

Established in 1990 by the National Council of Teachers of English to honor an outstanding informational book published in the preceding year

THE PURA BELPRÉ AWARD

Established in 1996 and cosponsored by the Association for Library Service to Children division of the American Library Association and the National Association to Promote Library Services to the Spanish Speaking to recognize a writer and illustrator of Latino or Latina background whose works affirm and celebrate the Latino experience

THE SCOTT O'DELL AWARD

Established in 1982 and presented by the O'Dell Award Committee to an American author who writes an outstanding tale of historical fiction for children or young adults that takes place in the New World

Nikki Grimes

Born: October 20, 1950

As a child, Nikki Grimes loved reading books. But few of the books she read had African American characters—people who looked like her or had the kinds of problems she faced in her home. In a way, she said, "The stories I read betrayed me." She decided to put things right. "When I grow up," she thought, "I'll write books about children who look and feel like me."

That's just what Grimes has done. She began writing when she was only six years old. Now she is the author of more than fifty books for children and young adults. Although she has written novels and nonfiction works, poetry is where she finds her strongest voice. Her characters reflect many of the feelings and situations that Grimes herself experienced growing up. Often her stories are about young African Americans trying to survive adolescence in New York City's urban settings.

GRIMES'S FAVORITE HOBBY IS KNITTING. IT'S A SKILL SHE PICKED UP IN SWEDEN. HER FAVORITE COLOR IS PURPLE, AND THE COLOR SHOWS UP IN MANY OF HER KNITTED CREATIONS.

Grimes knows this territory well. She was born in 1950 in New York City's Harlem district. Her father was a violinist, and her mother was a keypunch operator. Grimes's poems are alive with the rhythm and pulse of daily life in New York, and she often uses scenes from her childhood there. New York's buildings, neighborhoods, and city streets form the backdrop for many of her stories.

"The word, both written and spoken, has always held a special fascination for me. It seemed uncanny that words, spread across a page just so, had the power to transport me to another time and place. But they could. I spent many hours ensconced in the local library, reading—nay, devouring—book after book after book. Books were my soul's delight."

Growing up, Nikki and her family frequently moved from one city neighborhood to another. Her parents had a troubled marriage and separated many times. As a result, Nikki was shifted from one relative or foster home to another. That meant adjusting to different schools, leaving old friends, and making new friends. Grimes came to value friendship, a frequent theme in her writing. *Growin'*, her first children's book, is the story of Yolanda, a fifth-grade poet who makes friends with the school bully. Zuri and Danitra are unforgettable best friends in Grimes's Danitra Brown stories.

————

GRIMES WROTE SEVERAL BOOKS BASED ON WALT DISNEY CHARACTERS SUCH AS MICKEY MOUSE AND THE LITTLE MERMAID.

A Selected Bibliography of Grimes's Work

Oh, Brother! (2006)

Road to Paris (2006)

Welcome, Precious (2006)

Danitra Brown, Class Clown (2005)

Dark Sons (2005)

A Day with Daddy (2004)

Tai Chi Morning: Snapshots of China (2004)

What Is Goodbye? (2004)

Bronx Masquerade (2002)

C Is for City (2002)

Daintra Brown Leaves Town (2002)

Talkin' about Bessie: The Story of Aviator Elizabeth Coleman (2002)

When Daddy Prays (2002)

Is It Far to Zanzibar? (2000)

Stepping Out with Grandma Mac (2000)

Aneesa Lee and the Weaver's Gift (1999)

Jazmin's Notebook (1998)

It's Raining Laughter (1997)

Come Sunday (1996)

Meet Danitra Brown (1994)

Malcolm X: A Force for Change (1992)

Growin' (1977)

Grimes's Major Literary Awards

2003 Coretta Scott King Author Award
Bronx Masquerade

2003 Coretta Scott King Author Honor Book
Talkin' about Bessie: The Story of Aviator Elizabeth Coleman

1999 Coretta Scott King Author Honor Book
Jazmin's Notebook

Family and community relationships are also important themes for Grimes. LaTasha in *Come Sunday* is a little girl who loves the ritual of attending Paradise Baptist Church with her family. The poems in *Stepping Out with Grandma Mac* show the relationship between a young girl and her grandmother.

Grimes earned a degree in English literature from Rutgers University in New Jersey in 1974. After graduation she took some time to travel. She received a research grant from the Ford Foundation and spent a year in eastern Africa in the country of Tanzania. Her study of Tanzanian language and culture inspired her poetry collection *Is It Far to Zanzibar?* These poems focus on playful tales of Tanzanian children's daily lives. From 1977 to 1978, she worked for New York City's WBAI-FM radio station. There she wrote, produced, and hosted *The Kid Show.*

Grimes has received dozens of awards and honors for her uplifting but down-to-earth books. She now lives in Corona, California.

> *"Easy doesn't interest me. In art, and in life, I'm a sucker for a challenge. I like to take on work that frightens me, that I'm not sure I can pull off, that makes me dig deep."*

WHERE TO FIND OUT MORE ABOUT NIKKI GRIMES

BOOKS

Children's Literature Review. Vol. 42. Detroit: Gale, 1997.

Pendergast, Sara, and Tom Pendergast, eds. *St. James Guide to Children's Writers.* 5th ed. Detroit: St. James Press, 1999.

WEB SITES

THE CHILDREN'S BOOK COUNCIL
http://www.cbcbooks.org/yppw/celebrate/qa_nikkigrimes.html
For an interview with Nikki Grimes focusing on poetry

NIKKI GRIMES
http://www.nikkigrimes.com/
For a Web site devoted to Nikki Grimes featuring a biography, a list of books, poetry, tour information, questions, pictures, and much more

---

GRIMES HAS WRITTEN SEVERAL BOOKS UNDER THE NAME NAOMI MCMILLAN.

Margaret Peterson Haddix

Born: April 9, 1964

Margaret Peterson Haddix always wanted to be a storyteller. Now she's enjoying the career of her dreams. As a popular author of young-adult novels, she serves up tales of terror, intrigue, and triumph.

Margaret Peterson was born in 1964 in the town of Washington Court House, Ohio. It was a farming community, and her father ran the family farm. Like her sister and two brothers, Margaret split her time between farm chores and school.

Margaret enjoyed stories from an early age. Her father was an animated storyteller, and he entertained his kids with fantastic tales about their relatives. Margaret's mother, a nurse, was also a book lover. Margaret remembers her once saying, "Oh, I meant to

AS A CHILD, MARGARET DIDN'T THINK AN OHIO FARM GIRL COULD BECOME AN AUTHOR. SHE THOUGHT AUTHORS CAME ONLY FROM BIG, IMPORTANT CITIES.

clean house today, but I just had to see how this book ended."

Margaret loved reading books, too, and she thought it would be great to be a story-teller herself. She recalls that, as a child, she "longed for a career that I didn't actually believe real people got to do." That was a career as an author. Margaret began writing stories of her own, but she never told anyone about her dreams.

At Miami University in Oxford, Ohio, she majored in journalism, creative writing, and history. In 1983, she submitted a story to *Seventeen* magazine's annual fiction contest. She was delighted when she won an honorable mention. Finally, she began to

A Selected Bibliography of Haddix's Work

Among the Free (2006)
Among the Enemy (2005)
Double Identity (2005)
Among the Brave (2004)
Among the Barons (2003)
Escape from Memory (2003)
Among the Betrayed (2002)
Because of Anya (2002)
Among the Imposters (2001)
Takeoffs and Landings (2001)
Turnabout (2000)
Just Ella (1999)
Among the Hidden (1998)
Leaving Fishers (1997)
Don't You Dare Read This, Mrs. Dunphrey (1996)
Running Out of Time (1995)

> *"I feel like there are stories all around me, just waiting to be told."*

realize that she could become an author after all.

After graduation in 1986, she took a job as a copy editor for the *Fort Wayne Journal-Gazette* in Fort Wayne, Indiana. A few months later, she became a reporter for the *Indianapolis News* in Indianapolis, Indiana. In 1987, she married Doug Haddix. Meanwhile, she tried writing short stories, but there was never enough time to make them her main focus.

When the couple moved to Danville, Illinois, in 1991, Haddix finally quit newspaper work. She took a part-time teaching job at Danville Area Community College and spent her extra time writing. She began thinking about a newspaper article she once wrote about a historical village. She developed this idea into a science fiction novel about a family in the 1840s that discovers it is actually the same family depicted in a museum exhibit in the 1990s. The novel, *Running Out of Time*, was published in 1995.

By this time, the Haddix family included two small children, Meredith and Connor. Haddix had her hands full, but she went on to write more than a dozen young-adult novels. Their subjects range from religious cults to abused teens to futuristic worlds.

HADDIX RECEIVED HER DEGREE FROM MIAMI UNIVERSITY *SUMMA CUM LAUDE*, WHICH IS LATIN FOR "WITH HIGHEST HONORS."

Her Shadow Children books began with *Among the Hidden*. In this seven-book series, a group of kids try to survive in a bizarre and dangerous future world. *Leaving Fishers* explores a girl's descent into a religious cult. In *Just Ella*, Haddix puts a twist on the traditional Cinderella story. Ella, the heroine, plots a daring escape from her boring life with the prince.

As always, Haddix is working on her next novel. She and her family live in Powell, Ohio, a suburb of Columbus.

> *"Teenagers are naturally such good characters in books. They have great capacity for change, and they're often more interesting than adults."*

❧

WHERE TO FIND OUT MORE ABOUT MARGARET PETERSON HADDIX

WEB SITES

LIBRARY THINKQUEST
http://library.thinkquest.org/J0110073/Author.htmly
For a short biography and an interview with the author

SF SITE
http://www.sfsite.com/09b/amo41.htm
For a review of *Among the Hidden*

HADDIX GOT THE IDEAS FOR HER FIRST THREE BOOKS—*RUNNING OUT OF TIME*; *DON'T YOU DARE READ THIS, MRS. DUNPHREY*; AND *LEAVING FISHERS*—FROM NEWSPAPER STORIES.

Virginia Hamilton

Born: March 12, 1936
Died: February 19, 2002

Virginia Hamilton learned the art of storytelling as a young girl from listening to her grandfather, aunts, uncles, and parents. She used her love of storytelling to become an award-winning children's author. Her most popular books include *The House of Dies Drear; The Time-Ago Tales of Jahdu; The People Could Fly: American Black Folktales;* and *M. C. Higgins, the Great.*

Virginia Hamilton was born on March 12, 1936, in Yellow Springs, Ohio. Her family has lived in Ohio since the 1850s. Virginia's grandfather Levi Perry was a slave in Virginia. He escaped along the Underground Railroad and made it to Ohio. The story of his escape from slavery was often told in Virginia's family. "I grew up within the warmth of loving aunts and uncles, all reluctant farmers, but great storytellers," Hamilton noted.

VIRGINIA HAMILTON WAS GIVEN THE NAME VIRGINIA AS A WAY TO REMEMBER THE STATE WHERE HER GRANDFATHER HAD ESCAPED FROM SLAVERY.

Virginia loved school and did well at her studies. She began writing stories as a young girl and read as many books as she could. Virginia was very active in school. She participated in public speaking, sang at public events, and was captain of the girls' basketball team. As a high-school student, she wrote a play that was performed at the school.

Hamilton received a scholarship to study writing at Antioch College. She studied there for three years before transferring to Ohio State University. She went on to study at a school in New York where she met a young poet named Arnold Adoff. They married in 1960.

"There is no clear way to explain how it is that I never cease having new ideas for books nor the desire to work so intensely at writing them. But as raising a family and keeping up a working farm with my father was my mother's focus and heart, so writing is mine."

Hamilton took many jobs to earn money while she tried to get her writing published. She worked as an accountant, a receptionist, and a singer in a nightclub. Finally, a friend in the publishing business suggested that she expand a short story she had written into a children's book. This story later became her first book, *Zeely*, which was published in 1967. Soon after the book was published, Hamilton and her husband moved back to Ohio to live near her family.

HAMILTON WAS A BIG FAN OF FROGS—SHE COLLECTED STATUES OF FROGS AND STUFFED FROGS AND WAS EVEN FAMOUS FOR TELLING "FROG JOKES."

A Selected Bibliography of Hamilton's Work

Time Pieces: The Book of Times (2002)

The Girl Who Spun Gold (2000)

Second Cousins (1998)

Her Stories: African American Folktales, Fairy Tales, and True Tales (1995)

Many Thousand Gone: African Americans form Slavery to Freedom (1993)

Cousins (1990)

The Dark Way: Stories From the Spirit World (1990)

The Bells of Christmas (1989)

Anthony Burns: The Defeat and Triumph of a Fugitive Slave (1988)

In the Beginning: Creation Stories from around the World (1988)

Junius over Far (1985)

The People Could Fly: American Black Folktales (1985)

A Little Love (1984)

The Magical Adventures of Pretty Pearl (1983)

Sweet Whispers, Brother Rush (1982)

Justice and Her Brothers (1978)

M. C. Higgins, the Great (1974)

The Planet of Junior Brown (1972)

W. E. B. Du Bois: A Biography (1972)

The Time-Ago Tales of Jahdu (1969)

The House of Dies Drear (1968)

Zeely (1967)

Hamilton's Major Literary Awards

Virginia Hamilton is one of the most-honored authors of children's books. Due to space constraints, only her major literary awards dating back to 1990 are listed below. For a complete list, please visit Hamilton's Web site at *http://www.virginiahamilton.com/pages/awards.htm*

1996 Coretta Scott King Author Award
   Her Stories: African American Folktales, Fairy Tales, and True Tales

1995 Laura Ingalls Wilder Award

1994 Carter G. Woodson Outstanding Merit Book
   Many Thousand Gone: African Americans from Slavery to Freedom

1992 Hans Christian Andersen Medal for Authors

1990 Coretta Scott King Author Honor Book
   The Bells of Christmas

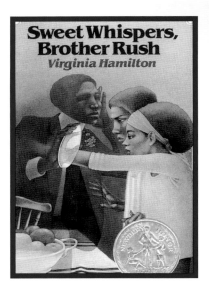

In her books, Hamilton used African American characters and emphasized many elements of black history in the United States. Her memories and the experiences she had as a young child are an important part of her books. Because she had such a strong connection to her family, most of her books include a strong sense of family.

Along with writing picture books for children and novels for young adults, Hamilton wrote biographies of famous African Americans for a young audience. She also edited collections of folktales. Hamilton lived with her husband on her family's land in southern Ohio until her death on February 19, 2002.

> *"My greatest pleasure is sitting down and weaving a tale out of the mystery of my past and present. I'm only thankful that children like my stories as well, my own children included."*

WHERE TO FIND OUT MORE ABOUT VIRGINIA HAMILTON

BOOKS

McElmeel, Sharron L. *100 Most Popular Children's Authors: Biographical Sketches and Bibliographies.* Englewood, Colo.: Libraries Unlimited, 1999.

Mikkelsen, Nina. *Virginia Hamilton.* New York: Twayne, 1994.

Rockman, Connie C., ed. *The Ninth Book of Junior Authors and Illustrators.* New York: H. W. Wilson Company, 2004.

Wheeler, Jill C. *Virginia Hamilton.* Minneapolis: Abdo & Daughters, 1997.

WEB SITES

DESCRIPTIVE WRITING WITH VIRGINIA HAMILTON
http://teacher.scholastic.com/writewit/diary/
Learn step-by-step how to write descriptive prose

VIRGINIA HAMILTON HOME PAGE
http://www.virginiahamilton.com/
For an autobiographical account by Virginia Hamilton, book information, and a photo gallery

A TRIP HAMILTON AND HER HUSBAND TOOK TO SPAIN AND NORTH AFRICA GREATLY INFLUENCED HER WRITING, ESPECIALLY *ZEELY.*

Joyce Hansen

Born: October 18, 1942

For years, Joyce Hansen worked as a teacher in the New York City public schools. When she began her career as a writer, she discovered how much she had learned from her students. Years of working with young people gave her insight into the ways of children. "All of my books were inspired by having the opportunity to meet so many young people in my teaching career," Hansen says. "I write realistic fiction about people and places that I know."

Joyce Hansen was born on October 18, 1942, in New York City. Both her mother and her father helped shape Joyce's desire to become a writer. Her mother, Lilian, passed on to Joyce a love for books and reading. Her father, Austin, taught her the art of storytelling. He liked to delight Joyce and

HANSEN TAUGHT IN PUBLIC SCHOOLS FOR TWENTY-TWO YEARS.

his other children with stories of his boyhood in the West Indies and his days as a young man in Harlem in the 1920s.

Hansen graduated from Pace University in 1972. She later earned a master's degree from New York University. In 1973, Hansen began teaching in the New York City public schools. She taught children with reading disabilities.

As a teacher, Hansen became convinced of the importance of stories in shaping young lives. "All children need sound, solid literature that relates to their own experiences and interests," she says.

As a writer, Hansen has tried to provide a realistic portrait of the lives of African

A Selected Bibliography of Hansen's Work

African Princess: The Amazing Lives of Africa's Royal Women (2004)

Freedom Roads: Searching for the Underground Railroad (2003)

One True Friend (2001)

Bury Me Not in a Land of Slaves: African-Americans in the Time of Reconstruction (2000)

The Heart Calls Home (1999)

Breaking Ground, Breaking Silence: The Story of New York's African Burial Ground (1998)

Women of Hope: African Americans Who Made a Difference (1998)

I Thought My Soul Would Rise and Fly: The Diary of Patsy, a Freed Girl (1997)

The Captive (1994)

Between Two Fires: Black Soldiers in the Civil War (1993)

Out from This Place (1988)

Which Way Freedom? (1986)

Yellow Bird and Me (1986)

Home Boy (1982)

The Gift-Giver (1980)

Hansen's Major Literary Awards

1999 Carter G. Woodson Honor Book
   Women of Hope: African Americans Who Made a Difference

1999 Coretta Scott King Author Honor Book
   Breaking Ground, Breaking Silence: The Story of New York's African Burial Ground

1998 Coretta Scott King Author Honor Book
   I Thought My Soul Would Rise and Fly: The Diary of Patsy, a Freed Girl

1995 Coretta Scott King Author Honor Book
   The Captive

1987 Coretta Scott King Author Honor Book
   Which Way Freedom?

> *"We must use our words to help our children acquire a richness of soul and spirit, so that perhaps one fine day we will learn to live with ourselves and one another in peace and harmony."*

American children. Some of her books take place in inner-city neighborhoods today. Others are set in the past and are based on historic events.

Hansen's first novel is set in a New York City neighborhood like the one in which she grew up. The novel is called *The Gift-Giver,* and it was published in 1980. It tells the story of a fifth-grader named Doris and her friendship with a shy classmate named Amir. In writing *The Gift-Giver,* Hansen drew on memories of her own childhood in New York.

Hansen wrote three more novels set in New York City. Then, for her next book, she tried a different approach. She wrote about African Americans in the American South during and after the Civil War (1861–1865).

Before she could write about the past, Hansen had to do research to learn about everyday life during the Civil War. "I was writing about a place and a time of which I had no direct knowledge," she explains. "I had to research my story very carefully because I wanted to be certain that my historical background was correct." *Which Way Freedom?* was named a Coretta Scott King Honor Book in 1987.

HANSEN GRADUATED FROM COLLEGE WHEN SHE WAS THIRTY YEARS OLD AND PUBLISHED HER FIRST BOOK WHEN SHE WAS THIRTY-EIGHT.

In 1994, Hansen published *The Captive,* which tells the story of a West African boy named Kofi who is sold into slavery in the United States in the late 1700s. *The Captive* was also named a Coretta Scott King Honor Book.

Today, Joyce Hansen lives with her husband in South Carolina. She works full-time on her writing.

❧

WHERE TO FIND OUT MORE ABOUT JOYCE HANSEN

BOOKS

Berger, Laura Standley, ed. *Twentieth-Century Children's Writers*, 4th ed. Detroit: St. James Press, 1995.

Collier, Laurie, and Joyce Nakamura, eds. *Major Authors and Illustrators for Children and Young Adults.* Detroit: Gale Research, 1993.

Rockman, Connie C., ed. *Eighth Book of Junior Authors and Illustrators.* New York: H. W. Wilson Company, 2000.

WEB SITES

JOYCE HANSEN HOME PAGE
http://www.joycehansen.com/
For biographical information and booklists

SCHOLASTIC AUTHORS ONLINE
http://www2.scholastic.com/teachers/authorsandbooks/authorstudies/
authorhome.jhtml?authorID=44&collateralID=5178&displayName=Biography
For an autobiographical sketch by Joyce Hansen, a booklist, and an interview transcript

———

ONE OF HANSEN'S BOOKS, *BREAKING GROUND, BREAKING SILENCE: THE STORY OF NEW YORK'S AFRICAN BURIAL GROUND,* TELLS THE STORY OF AN AFRICAN AMERICAN BURIAL GROUND IN NEW YORK CITY THAT DATES BACK TO COLONIAL TIMES.

James Haskins

Born: September 19, 1941
Died: July 6, 2005

James Haskins grew up in Alabama. When he was a young boy, African Americans were not treated well. They did not have the same rights as white people. When Haskins decided to become a writer, he remembered the hardships of his childhood. He is best known for his nonfiction books for children and young people. His most popular books include *The Picture Life of Malcolm X; Street Gangs: Yesterday and Today; The Story of Stevie Wonder;* and *Black Dance in America: A History through Its People.*

James Haskins was born on September 19, 1941, in Demopolis, Alabama. The town where he grew up was a segregated community.

THE 1984 FILM *THE COTTON CLUB* WAS BASED
ON ONE OF HASKINS'S ADULT NOVELS.

Black people were not allowed to do the same things as white people. There were many places where black people were not allowed to go.

James's family was poor, but he had a happy family life. Storytelling was a big part of his childhood. "My Aunt Cindy was the greatest story-teller who ever lived," Haskins noted. Her stories inspired Haskins to write about things that he experienced.

As a young boy, James loved to read. It was difficult for him to get books because African Americans were not allowed into the public library. His mother eventually got him an encyclo-pedia from the supermarket, buying one volume at a time.

"I knew exactly the kind of books I wanted to do—books about current events and books about important black people so that students could understand the larger world around them through books written at a level they could understand."

James attended a segregated elementary school. Only black children attended the school. The school did not have many books for students to read. Even though the school did not have new books or modern equipment, James had great respect for his teachers.

As a teenager, James moved to Boston, Massachusetts, with his mother. He did well in high school but decided to return to Alabama after graduation. Haskins went to college in Alabama for a short

WHEN HASKINS WROTE ABOUT THE MUSICIAN STEVIE WONDER, HE WAS ABLE TO MEET WONDER IN LOS ANGELES.

A Selected Bibliography of Haskins's Work

Africa: A Look Back (2007)

African Heroes (2005)

Toni Morrison: Telling a Tale Untold (2002)

Champion: The Story of Muhammad Ali (2001)

Carter G. Woodson: The Man Who Put "Black" in American History (2000)

Bayard Rustin: Behind the Scenes of the Civil Rights Movement (1997)

The Harlem Renaissance (1996)

The March on Washington (1993)

Outward Dreams: Black Inventors and Their Inventions (1991)

Black Music in America: A History through Its People (1987)

Lena Horne (1983)

Andrew Young, Man with a Mission (1979)

Barbara Jordan (1977)

The Story of Stevie Wonder (1976)

The Picture Life of Malcolm X (1975)

Street Gangs: Yesterday and Today (1974)

A Piece of the Power: Four Black Mayors (1972)

Haskins's Major Literary Awards

2001 Carter G. Woodson Honor Book
  Carter G. Woodson: The Man Who Put "Black" in American History

1998 Coretta Scott King Author Honor Book
  Bayard Rustin: Behind the Scenes of the Civil Rights Movement

1997 Carter G. Woodson Book Award
  The Harlem Renaissance

1994 Carter G. Woodson Book Award
  The March on Washington

1993 Carter G. Woodson Outstanding Merit Book
  Thurgood Marshall: A Life for Justice

1992 Carter G. Woodson Outstanding Merit Book
  Outward Dreams: Black Inventors and Their Inventions

1991 Coretta Scott King Author Honor Book
1988 Carter G. Woodson Book Award
  Black Music in America: A History through Its People

1984 Coretta Scott King Author Honor Book
  Lena Horne

1980 Carter G. Woodson Outstanding Merit Book
1980 Coretta Scott King Author Honor Book
  James Van DerZee: The Picture-Takin' Man

1980 Coretta Scott King Author Honor Book
  Andrew Young, Man with a Mission

1978 Coretta Scott King Author Honor Book
  Barbara Jordan

1977 Coretta Scott King Author Award
  The Story of Stevie Wonder

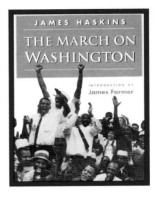

time. He was also involved in the civil rights movement in the South. He eventually attended universities in Washington, D.C., and New Mexico.

After finishing college, Haskins went to work for a stock brokerage firm. He didn't find the work very fulfilling, so he got a job as a special education teacher. The people he worked with encouraged him to keep a journal about his experiences as a teacher. His journal writing resulted in his first book, *Diary of a Harlem*

Schoolteacher. Publishers then asked Haskins to write books for children. He wrote more than one hundred nonfiction books for children and young people.

James Haskins also taught writing at several colleges and universities. He lived in Florida and taught at the University of Florida. James Haskins died at the age of sixty-three.

> *"Since my first major reading was the encyclopedia, this is probably another reason why I prefer nonfiction."*

WHERE TO FIND OUT MORE ABOUT JAMES HASKINS

BOOKS

Berger, Laura Standley, ed. *Twentieth-Century Young Adult Writers.* 1st ed. Detroit: St. James Press, 1994.

Something about the Author. Autobiography Series. Vol. 3. Detroit: Gale Research, 1978.

Sutherland, Zena. *Children & Books.* 9th ed. New York: Addison Wesley Longman, 1997.

WEB SITE

CHILDRENSLIT.COM
http://www.childrenslit.com/f_haskins.html
To read a biographical sketch of James Haskins and descriptions of some of his books

HASKINS WAS GUEST CURATOR FOR A SMITHSONIAN INSTITUTION TRAVELING EXHIBITION CALLED *THE JAZZ AGE IN PARIS,* WHICH OPENED IN WASHINGTON, D.C., IN 1997.

Kevin Henkes

Born: November 26, 1960

S ometimes adults do know just how you feel. In the books of Kevin Henkes, the children are not perfect. They have the problems that many kids face. They sometimes feel lonely or too messy or a little awkward. The bespectacled Henkes seems to know just how painful childhood can be. He also captures the humor of growing up and the

sense of intrigue in a child's day-to-day life. Ever since Henkes was a child he wanted to be an artist, which made him a little different from most of his classmates.

Kevin Henkes was born on November 26, 1960, in Racine, Wisconsin, the son of Barney and Beatrice Henkes. He has three brothers and a sister.

As a child, Kevin could often be found drawing, coloring, and painting. He loved

KEVIN HENKES'S *A WEEKEND WITH WENDELL* WAS NAMED A CHILDREN'S CHOICE BOOK BY THE CHILDREN'S BOOK COUNCIL AND THE INTERNATIONAL READING ASSOCIATION.

his art classes, and he says that everyone thought of him as an artist, even at a young age. He seems never to have doubted it himself.

When Henkes was just nineteen years old, he flew to New York City with his drawings and a map of the city. The map must have led him to the right place, for he landed a contract that led to his first book, which he called *All Alone*. Henkes says he will never forget that day in New York when his

> *"I'm a very lucky person. I've known for a very long time that I wanted to be an artist and a writer— and that's exactly what I do for a living."*

A Selected Bibliography of Henkes's Work

Good Day (2007)
Lilly's Big Day (2005)
Kitten's First Full Moon (2004)
Olive's Ocean (2003)
Wemberly's Ice Cream Star (2003)
Owen's Marshmallow Chick (2002)
Sheila Rae's Peppermint Stick (2001)
Wemberly Worried (2000)
The Birthday Room (1999)
Oh! (Text only, 1999)
Circle Dogs (Text only, 1998)
Sun & Spoon (1998)
Lilly's Purple Plastic Purse (1996)
Protecting Marie (1995)
Owen (1993)
Words of Stone (1992)
Chrysanthemum (1991)
Julius, the Baby of the World (1990)
Shhhh (1989)
Chester's Way (1988)
Sheila Rae, the Brave (1987)
Two under Par (1987)
Grandpa & Bo (1986)
A Weekend with Wendell (1986)
Bailey Goes Camping (1985)
Return to Sender (1984)
Margaret & Taylor (1983)
Clean Enough (1982)
All Alone (1981)

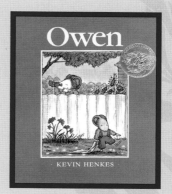

Henkes's Major Literary Awards

2005 Caldecott Medal
    Kitten's First Full Moon
2004 Newbery Honor Book
    Olive's Ocean

1994 Boston Globe-Horn Book Picture Book Honor Book
1994 Caldecott Honor Book
    Owen

career began. At the time, he was a freshman in college, studying at the University of Wisconsin at Madison.

After college, he married Laura Dronzek. Henkes has been a writer and illustrator ever since.

A young character—who is often a mouse—is usually the focus of one of Henkes's picture books. His characters have distinctive personalities with real problems. His readers find out how Sophie learned to like Wendell, what Chester's way is, how Julius becomes the baby of the world, and why Wemberly worried.

> *"When I was younger, I wondered about authors and illustrators. What did they look like? Where did they live? Did they have families? How old were they? And now I am one myself. Sometimes it's hard to believe."*

> *"Even if something traumatic happens to one of my characters, I like to have my stories end on a hopeful note. That's my gift to the reader."*

In Henkes's picture books, the child's world is seen through the child's eyes. Through his words, illustrations, and humor, Henkes has shown that although he has grown into an adult, he can still live in the world of a child. Henkes has also written several young adult novels.

Kevin Henkes lives with his wife and children in Madison, Wisconsin. He works on his books almost every day.

IN 2000, HENKES WAS INVITED TO WRITE THE INTRODUCTION TO STORIES ABOUT BABAR, THE WORLD'S MOST FAMOUS ELEPHANT. IT APPEARS IN *BONJOUR, BABAR! THE SIX UNABRIDGED CLASSICS BY THE CREATOR OF BABAR.*

❧

Where to Find Out More About Kevin Henkes

Books

Holtz, Sally Holmes, ed. *Sixth Book of Junior Authors & Illustrators.*
New York: H. W. Wilson Company, 1989.

Silvey, Anita, ed. *Children's Books and Their Creators.*
Boston: Houghton Mifflin, 1995.

Web Sites

Educational Paperback Association
http://edupaperback.org/showauth.cfm?authid=31
To read an autobiographical sketch by and a booklist for Kevin Henkes

HarperChildrens.com
http://www.harperchildrens.com/catalog/author_xml.asp?authorid=16903
To read a brief biographical sketch of Kevin Henkes, and to find
links to sites with information on each of his books

Kevin Henkes Home Page
http://www.kevinhenkes.com
To read an interview with Henkes, to find out more about
Henkes's characters, and to download book-related games

———

Kevin Henkes worked with his wife, Laura Dronzek, on one book.
Oh! was written by Henkes and illustrated by Dronzek.

Marguerite Henry

Born: April 13, 1902
Died: November 26, 1997

arguerite Henry wrote many books about dogs, birds, and even mules. But her most famous book is about a horse named Misty and the two orphaned children who are drawn to her.

Misty of Chincoteague was published in 1947 and has since sold more than a million copies. It won many awards and honors and is considered a classic of children's literature. Although Henry wrote about animals in the great outdoors and lived much of her life on a farm, she was born and raised in a city.

She was born Marguerite Breithaupt on April 13, 1902, in Milwaukee, Wisconsin. Marguerite's

ONE OF MARGUERITE HENRY'S BOOKS, *KING OF THE WIND*, WON THE NEWBERY MEDAL. *KING OF THE WIND* TELLS THE STORY OF AN ARABIAN STALLION IN THE 1700S WHO STARTED THE LINE OF TODAY'S THOROUGHBRED RACEHORSES.

father owned a publishing company. When she was a little girl, Marguerite liked to go to her father's business on Saturdays and watch books being printed. One day when she was ten, her father let Marguerite look at a set of proofs—the pages that show how a book will look once it is printed. She decided on the spot that she would become a writer.

Marguerite's father bought her a writing table and writing supplies, and Marguerite began working on her dream. When she was eleven, she submitted an essay about autumn to a popular women's magazine. The magazine printed the essay, and Marguerite's writing career had begun.

While attending Milwaukee State Teachers College, she continued writing, and she also acted in plays. After she graduated, she married a salesman named Sidney Crocker Henry.

The newlywed couple bought a farm in Wayne, Illinois, and settled there. Marguerite Henry began writing professionally. She sold articles and stories to magazines such as *Reader's Digest,* the *Saturday Evening Post,* and *Forum.*

Henry published her first book for children in 1940. It was called *Auno and Tauno: A Story of*

> *"Stepping softly in the sand, the burro sneaked behind the prospector and playfully butted him up from his crouching position. The old man spun around, his face lighting with joy. 'Brighty!' he shouted happily."*
> —*from* **Brighty of the Grand Canyon**

HENRY'S BOOKS HAVE BEEN TRANSLATED INTO SEVERAL LANGUAGES, INCLUDING URDU, ARABIC, AND AFRIKAANS.

King of the Wind

The Story of the Godolphin Arabian

By MARGUERITE HENRY • Illustrated by WESLEY DENNIS

A Selected Bibliography of Henry's Work

Brown Sunshine of Sawdust Valley (1996)
Misty's Twilight (1992)
San Domingo, the Medicine Hat Stallion (1972)
Mustang, Wild Spirit of the West (1966)
Stormy, Misty's Foal (1963)
Five O'Clock Charlie (1962)
Black Gold (1957)
Brighty of the Grand Canyon (1953)
Album of Horses (1951)
Born to Trot (1950)
Sea Star: Orphan of Chincoteague (1949)
King of the Wind (1948)
Misty of Chincoteague (1947)
Justin Morgan Had a Horse (1945)
Auno and Tauno: A Story of Finland (1940)

Henry's Major Literary Awards

1949 Newbery Medal
   King of the Wind

1948 Newbery Honor Book
   Misty of Chincoteague

1946 Newbery Honor Book
   Justin Morgan Had a Horse

Finland. In 1945, her book *Justin Morgan Had a Horse* was published. It told the story of the founding of the Morgan breed of horses in Vermont. Henry worked with illustrator Wesley Dennis on the book. Henry and Dennis worked well together and eventually, they worked together on some twenty books.

Their second book was their most successful. It was *Misty of Chincoteague.* The book is set on Chincoteague Island, off the coasts of Virginia and Maryland. Henry based the story on a real horse that she found when she visited the island. She even brought the real Misty home to live on her Illinois farm with her for several years. *Misty of Chincoteague* won many major prizes for children's literature. Its honors include the Lewis Carroll Shelf Award, one of publishing's most important prizes.

> *"The ponies were exhausted and their coats were heavy with water, but they were free, free, free!"*
> —*from* Misty of Chincoteague

Henry continued to write stories about Misty for nearly fifty years. In all, she wrote more than fifty books. Marguerite Henry died on November 26, 1997.

∾

WHERE TO FIND OUT MORE ABOUT MARGUERITE HENRY

BOOKS

Collins, David. *Write a Book for Me: The Story of Marguerite Henry.*
Greensboro, N.C.: Morgan Reynolds, 1999.

Henry, Marguerite. *A Pictorial Life Story of Misty.*
Chicago: Rand McNally, 1976.

Silvey, Anita, ed. *The Essential Guide to Children's Books and Their Creators.*
Boston: Houghton Mifflin Company, 2002.

WEB SITE

GREENVILLE PUBLIC LIBRARY: JUVENILE
BOOKS AUTHOR OF THE MONTH
http://www.yourlibrary.ws/childrens_webpage/j-author42001.html
To read a detailed biographical sketch of Marguerite Henry

———

A LIFE-SIZE STATUE OF THE REAL-LIFE MISTY STANDS ON CHINCOTEAGUE ISLAND.

Karen Hesse

Born: August 29, 1952

Many of Karen Hesse's novels take place in the distant past and in faraway places. Before she writes her novels, Hesse does careful research to help her understand everyday life in other times and places. "I love research," she says. "I love dipping into another time and place."

Karen Hesse was born on August 29, 1952, in Baltimore, Maryland. As a child, she was often ill. She found comfort in reading. Her favorite reading spot was a hideaway in the limbs of an apple tree in her backyard. Karen spent hours there reading her favorite stories. She also was a frequent visitor to the Enoch Pratt Free Library near her home. She began reading Dr. Seuss

THE IDEA FOR THE NOVEL *THE MUSIC OF DOLPHINS* CAME FROM AN INTERVIEW HESSE HEARD ON THE RADIO.

books at the library and formed a fascination with storytelling that has lasted all her life.

By the time Karen was a teenager, she was reading books written for adults. One of those books had an especially strong impact on her. It was John Hersey's *Hiroshima,* which tells the story of the dropping of an atomic bomb on a Japanese city during World War II (1939–1945). Many years later, Hesse wrote her own novel on a similar topic. *Phoenix Rising* is about the horrors of a nuclear disaster.

In high school, Karen became interested in acting. She joined an acting group and performed in amateur productions. Later, she studied drama

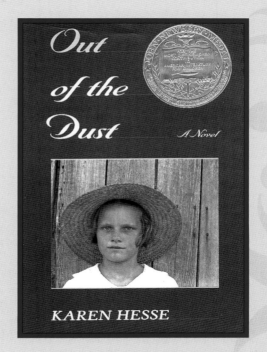

A Selected Bibliography of Hesse's Work

Young Hans Christian Andersen (2005)
Cats in Krasinski Square (2004)
Stone Lamp: A Hanukkah Collection (2002)
Witness (2001)
Stowaway (2000)
Come On, Rain (1999)
A Light in the Storm: The Civil War Diary of Amelia Martin (1999)
Just Juice (1998)
Out of the Dust (1997)
The Music of Dolphins (1996)
A Time of Angels (1995)
Phoenix Rising (1994)
Sable (1994)
Lavender (1993)
Lester's Dog (1993)
Poppy's Chair (1993)
Letters from Rifka (1992)
Wish on a Unicorn (1991)

Hesse's Major Literary Awards

1998 Newbery Medal
1998 Scott O'Dell Award
   Out of the Dust

at Towson State College in Maryland for two years. However, she cut her studies short to marry Randy Hesse.

Eventually, Hesse finished college at the University of Maryland. She graduated in 1975 with a degree in English. While attending the university, Hesse began writing and giving readings of her poetry.

After graduation, Hesse worked at a series of jobs. She was a secretary, a librarian, a substitute teacher, and a proofreader—a person who checks for mistakes in books and other printed material. Hesse and her husband settled in Vermont and had two daughters—Kate born in 1979, and Rachel, born in 1982.

> *"Writing is not easy. I work for long hours and sometimes all that work disappoints me and I throw it out and begin again."*

Hesse's first novel, *Wish on a Unicorn,* was published in 1991. The following year, Hesse published *Letters from Rifka.* It tells the story of a young Jewish girl in Russia in the early 1900s. To escape the brutality of war, her family leaves Russia to live in the United States. However, Rifka becomes separated from her family and has to find her own way to the United States.

In 1997, Hesse published *Out of the Dust.* The novel takes place in Oklahoma during the 1930s. A drought destroyed farms all across the middle of the United States during those years. Rich soil was turned into

HESSE WORKED IN THE COLLEGE LIBRARY TO HELP PAY FOR HER EDUCATION.

dust, and the entire middle of the country was called the Dust Bowl. Hesse's novel tells how a father and daughter survive the terrible poverty of the time. Hesse won the 1998 Newbery Medal for *Out of the Dust.*

Karen Hesse still lives in Vermont with her family. She continues to write for young people, whom she calls "the most challenging, demanding, and rewarding audiences."

◆

WHERE TO FIND OUT MORE ABOUT KAREN HESSE

BOOKS

Rockman, Connie C., ed. *Eighth Book of Junior Authors and Illustrators.* New York: H. W. Wilson Company, 2000.

Silvey, Anita, ed. *The Essential Guide to Children's Books and Their Creators.* Boston: Houghton Mifflin Company, 2002.

Something about the Author. Vol. 74. Detroit: Gale Research, 1993.

WEB SITES

EDUCATIONAL PAPERBACK ASSOCIATION
http://edupaperback.org/showauth.cfm?authid=56
To read an autobiographical sketch by and a booklist for Karen Hesse

KIDSREADS.COM
http://www.kidsreads.com/authors/au-hesse-karen.asp
To read autobiographical information

HESSE RISES AT 5 A.M. EACH DAY TO BEGIN WRITING.

Carl Hiaasen

Born: March 12, 1953

Saving the environment is a worthwhile cause. But it can lead to dangerous adventures—especially for kids. That's the message Carl Hiaasen conveys in his young-adult novels.

Carl Hiaasen was born in 1953 in Plantation, Florida, a suburb of Fort Lauderdale. He grew up there on the edge of the Everglades, a vast marshland in southern Florida. As a child, Carl loved exploring the woods and swamps around his home.

When Carl was four, he learned to read by poring over the sports section of the *Miami Herald*, the major newspaper in Miami, Florida. From an early age, he knew he wanted to be a writer.

AS A TEENAGER, CARL HIAASEN WORKED AS A JANITOR IN A VETERINARIAN'S OFFICE AND IN A DAY CARE CENTER.

He got a typewriter when he was
six, and he used it to type up a
newspaper about local sports for
the neighborhood kids.

> *"I've gotten hundreds and hundreds of letters from kids. They like the fact that these kids [in my books] make the difference—and that adults don't ride in at the last scene and save the day."*

After graduating from high
school in 1970, Hiaasen married
Connie Lyford and enrolled in
Emory University in Atlanta, Georgia. The next year, the couple's son,
Scott, arrived. In 1972, Hiaasen transferred to the University of Florida
in Gainesville. He graduated in 1974 with a degree in journalism.

Hiaasen joined the *Miami Herald* in 1976. His work as a reporter
coincided with his love for Florida's natural beauty. As an investiga-
tive journalist, he targeted developers who made shady deals to destroy
natural areas in order to build housing and shopping districts.

In the 1980s, Hiaasen began writing adult mystery novels. Like his
newspaper articles, they explored the crime and corruption surrounding greedy land developers. Meanwhile, Hiaasen's first marriage ended
in divorce. In 1999, he married restaurant manager Fenia Clizer, who
had a son named Ryan. Soon the couple's son, Quinn, was born.

In 2002, Hiaasen wrote his first young-adult novel, *Hoot*. Like
his adult novels, this one revolves around environmental themes. It's

WHEN HIAASEN WAS BORN IN 1953, HIS HOMETOWN OF PLANTATION HAD A
POPULATION OF FEWER THAN FIVE HUNDRED. TODAY, MORE THAN 85,000 PEOPLE
LIVE IN PLANTATION.

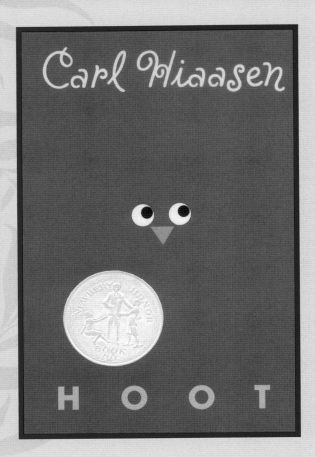

A Selected Bibliography of Hiaasen's Work
Flush (2005)
Hoot (2002)

Hiaasen's Major Literary Award
2003 Newbery Honor Book
  Hoot

about a group of school kids who try to stop construction crews from destroying the habitat of a colony of burrowing owls.

Hoot takes place in an area much like Hiaasen's childhood neighborhood. He had once watched helplessly as bulldozers tore through some burrowing owls' homes. "I remember watching them be wiped out," he recalled, "and the idea that my friends and I couldn't stop it." *Hoot* was made into a movie that was released in 2006.

Hiassen's next young-adult novel, *Flush*, appeared in 2005. It follows a teenage boy and his sister who decide to take action against a casino boat that's dumping waste into Florida's waters.

The environment remains a personal issue for Hiaasen. He remembers a dirt road where he and his friends used to ride their bikes. Now that road is an eight-lane highway with shopping malls on either side. Today, Hiaasen and his family enjoy nature in Islamorada, a fishing village in the Florida Keys.

> *"There is a unique and unforgettable feeling you get in the pit of your stomach when you turn a corner and that place [you enjoyed as a child] is not there."*

WHERE TO FIND OUT MORE ABOUT CARL HIAASEN

WEB SITES

CARL HIAASEN
http://www.carlhiaasen.com
For a biography and FAQs about his books for adults and children

RANDOM HOUSE
http://www.randomhouse.com/features/hiaasen/author.html
To read a biography and listen to an interview of Carl Hiaasen

TIME FOR KIDS
http://www.timeforkids.com/TFK/news/story/0,6260,1138836,00.html
For an interview with the author

HOOT IS BEING USED IN FLORIDA'S SEVENTH-GRADE SCIENCE AND SOCIAL STUDIES CLASSES TO COMBINE THE STUDY OF LITERATURE AND ENVIRONMENTAL SCIENCE.

Eric Hill

Born: September 7, 1927

Eric Hill discovered by accident that children like to look behind the flaps of books. He was working on an advertising project that had movable flaps, and his young son kept opening the panels to see what was behind them. Just as children like to open the doors of cupboards to see inside, they also like to open the flaps of Hill's children's books and discover all sorts of funny creatures staring back at them. The book is almost like a toy, and some books even have movable panels so that children can create their own designs and pictures.

Eric Hill was born in London, England, on September 7, 1927. He liked drawing from an early age. After World War II (1939–1945)

ERIC HILL'S STORIES ABOUT SPOT THE DOG WERE MADE INTO A TELEVISION SHOW CALLED *ADVENTURES OF SPOT* BY THE BRITISH BROADCASTING CORPORATION.

began in 1939, Eric was taken away from London to avoid German air force planes that pummeled the city with bombs. Like many other children, though, he found life in the countryside dull compared to life in London. Soon he returned to the city.

Eric became fascinated by the fighters and bombers that flew over London. He learned the names of the planes and sketched them on his drawing pad. Later in the war, he got a job as a messenger and a sweeper at an art studio in London. One of the artists introduced him to cartooning, and Eric began to develop the simple lines and childlike style of his drawings.

From 1945 until 1948, Hill served in the Royal Air Force. After leaving the military, he began his career as an illustrator and designer for advertisements.

Hill was married from 1950 until 1972 to Barbara Hobson, and in 1973 to Gillian McCarthy. He has two children, Jane and Christopher.

It was Christopher's curiosity that sparked Hill's interest in re-designing children's books. And it was for Christopher that Hill began to draw a puppy named Spot. Hill had found that many children's

"I consider myself very fortunate indeed to have created a character which has captured the imagination and enthusiasm of so many children worldwide. They are my family, and Spot belongs to them all."

THE SPOT BOOKS HAVE BEEN TRANSLATED INTO SIXTY-FIVE LANGUAGES. PART OF THE REASON THAT SPOT IS IN SUCH DEMAND IS THAT THE STORIES ARE SIMPLE AND EASY TO UNDERSTAND IN ANY LANGUAGE.

Where's Spot?

Eric Hill

A Selected Bibliography of Hill's Work

Spot's Jigsaw Puzzle (2004)

Spot's Little Book of Fun at the Beach (2003)

Spot's Little Book of Fun in the Garden (2003)

Spot's Treasure Hunt (2002)

Spot Goes Splash! And Other Stories (2000)

Good Night, Spot (1999)

Spot's Favorite Baby Animals (1997)

Spot's Walk in the Woods (1993)

Spot at Home (1991)

Spot Goes to the Circus (1986)

Spot at Play (1985)

Baby Bear's Bedtime (1984)

My Pets (1983)

Where's Spot? (1980)

books were unsuitable for small children, so he kept Spot's adventures simple. The reader follows Spot on his first walk, to his first birthday party, and to school. Children can follow Spot through the same adventures that they themselves have. Indeed, the Spot books seem to have filled a void in children's literature—by telling simple stories that even very young children can grasp. Hill has also been praised for depicting Spot with simple lines, much the way a child would draw.

"I love dogs, and it seemed that the easiest thing for me to do was to draw something I loved."

Since making Spot one of the most famous dogs in literature, Eric Hill has moved to California. There, surrounded by a large collection of metal toys, he continues to write.

⟨❧⟩

WHERE TO FIND OUT MORE ABOUT ERIC HILL

BOOKS

Children's Literature Review. Vol. 13. Detroit: Gale Research, 1987.

Holtze, Sally Holmes, ed. *Sixth Book of Junior Authors & Illustrators.* New York: H. W. Wilson Company, 1989

Silvey, Anita, ed. *The Essential Guide to Children's Books and Their Creators.* Boston: Houghton Mifflin Company, 2002.

WEB SITE

THE OFFICIAL SPOT WEB SITE
http://www.funwithspot.com/
To take an interactive tour of Spot's world, including trips to the farm and the beach

----

WHERE'S SPOT?—ERIC HILL'S FIRST SPOT BOOK—WOULD PROBABLY HAVE NEVER BEEN PUBLISHED IF A FRIEND HADN'T TAKEN A SAMPLE OF IT TO A BOOK FAIR IN FRANKFURT, GERMANY. HILL HADN'T SERIOUSLY THOUGHT ABOUT PUBLISHING IT.

S. E. Hinton

Born: July 22, 1948

E. Hinton changed the world of young-adult fiction with her gritty, hard-boiled teen novels. She wrote her first and most popular book, *The Outsiders*, when she was only a teenager herself.

Susan Eloise Hinton was born in 1948 in Tulsa, Oklahoma. Her family called her Susie. Susie was a tomboy, and she loved riding horses. She began writing stories when she was young.

Susie didn't really enjoy the young-adult books available when she was in high school. In her opinion, they were too sweet and innocent. The characters' biggest problems seemed to revolve around dating boys and getting ready for the prom. Susie preferred realistic stories

HINTON USUALLY WRITES HER BOOKS WITH A PEN OR PENCIL. SHE LATER TYPES THEM INTO A COMPUTER.

about teenage life as she knew it. After a friend of hers was brutally beaten, she began writing *The Outsiders*, a story about teen gangs.

When Susie was a sophomore in high school, her father was hospitalized with a brain tumor. As his condition worsened, she withdrew into her writing project. Sadly, her father died when she was a junior. She finished the book around the same time, and it was published in 1967.

> *"If you want to be a writer, I have two pieces of advice. One is to be a reader. . . . The other piece of advice is 'Just do it!' Don't think about it, don't agonize—sit down and write."*

Because *The Outsiders* was written from a boy's point of view, Hinton's publisher suggested that she use her initials, S. E., instead of her full name. At first, *The Outsiders* was slow to catch on with the public because its subject matter was so unusual. But teenagers around the country gradually heard about the book, and it went on to sell millions of copies.

Hinton enrolled in the University of Tulsa and majored in education. In college, she read books by a number of famous authors. Then she decided to go back and read *The Outsiders* once again. She was mortified. "I thought it was the worst piece of trash I'd ever seen," she says.

Hinton met David Inhofe while she was in college, and after graduation in 1970, they married. It didn't take long for Hinton to realize

---

HINTON DOESN'T MAKE PERSONAL APPEARANCES AS AN AUTHOR BECAUSE SHE DOESN'T ENJOY TRAVELING OR SPEAKING IN PUBLIC.

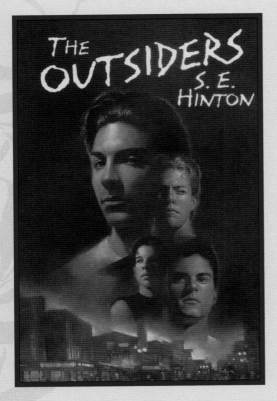

A Selected Bibliography of Hinton's Work

Big David, Little David (1995)

The Puppy Sister (1995)

Taming the Star Runner (1988)

Tex (1979)

Rumble Fish (1975)

That Was Then, This Is Now (1971)

The Outsiders (1967)

that she was not cut out to be a teacher. Encouraged by her husband, she began working on a second novel. *That Was Then, This Is Now* was published in 1971. More novels appeared over the next several years.

In the early 1980s, Hinton worked with Hollywood filmmakers to turn several of her books into movies. The movie *Tex* came out in 1982. Both *The Outsiders* and *Rumble Fish* were released as movies in 1983. *That Was Then, This Is Now* hit theaters in 1985.

"I remember exactly what it was like to be a teenager that nobody listened to or paid attention to or wanted around."

Hinton's son, Nicholas David, was born in 1983. While raising her little boy, she got the ideas for two books for younger children. Both *Big David, Little David* and *The Puppy Sister* were published in 1995.

Hinton lives in Tulsa, where she still enjoys horseback riding.

WHERE TO FIND OUT MORE ABOUT S. E. HINTON

BOOKS

Children's Literature Review. Vol. 23. Detroit: Gale, 1991.

Daly, Jay. *Presenting S. E. Hinton*. Boston: Twayne, 1987.

Silvey, Anita, ed. *The Essential Guide to Children's Books and Their Creators.*
Boston: Houghton Mifflin Company, 2002.

Sutherland, Zena. *Children and Books*. 9th ed. Boston: Allyn & Bacon, 1997.

WEB SITES

RANDOM HOUSE
http://www.randomhouse.com/author/results.pperl?authorid=13074&view=sml_sptlght
To read an extensive biography of the author and her work

S. E. HINTON
http://www.sehinton.com/
For a biography and list of books by Susan Eloise Hinton

WIRED FOR SOUND
http://wiredforbooks.org/sehinton/
To listen to an interview with S. E. Hinton

THE MAIN CHARACTERS IN ALL OF HINTON'S BOOKS (EXCEPT *THE PUPPY SISTER*) ARE BOYS.

Tana Hoban

Born: c. 1917
Born: January 27, 2006

Tana Hoban was fascinated by familiar objects. They were everyday things—a bowl, a spoon, a sunflower. But have you seen them like this before? Her photograph of a bowl brought out its beauty. She turned her camera to the spoon, and its curving body took on life. Everyday objects that we hardly noticed as we handled them were given their own personality in the photographs of Tana Hoban.

Tana Hoban was born in Philadelphia, Pennsylvania. Her family moved to a country house in Lansdale, Pennsylvania, before Tana started school. In the countryside, she slept on a screened porch until the weather turned too cold. She helped her family raise pigeons and bees, tend the garden, and feed the chickens.

HOBAN'S PHOTOGRAPHS HAVE BEEN EXHIBITED IN THE UNITED STATES AND FRANCE. THEY ARE PART OF THE NEW YORK MUSEUM OF MODERN ART'S COLLECTION.

On weekends, she studied art, and found that she was quite good at it. Tana was so good that she won a scholarship to Moore College of Art. Following graduation, she went to Europe to work on her paintings.

When Hoban returned from Europe, she began a promising career as an illustrator. Her work was featured in magazines and in advertisements. It was during this time that she met a photographer named Edward Gallob.

Gallob not only gave her her first camera, he also became her husband. They had a daughter, Miela.

Although the couple later divorced—and Hoban would marry John G. Morris—

A Selected Bibliography of Hoban's Work

Cubes, Cones, Cylinders, & Spheres (2000)
I Wonder (1999)
Construction Zone (1997)
Just Look (1996)
Animal, Vegetable, or Mineral? (1995)
What Is That? (1994)
Black on White (1993)
All about Where (1991)
Exactly the Opposite (1990)
Shadows and Reflections (1990)
Panda, Panda (1986)
A Children's Zoo (1985)
Is It Larger? Is It Smaller? (1985)
1, 2, 3 (1985)
Round and Round and Round (1983)
Take Another Look (1981)
Is It Red? Is It Yellow? Is It Blue? (1978)
Where Is It? (1978)
Push, Pull, Empty, Full: A Book of Opposites (1972)
Look Again! (1971)
Shapes and Things (1970)

Hoban's Major Literary Awards

1985 Boston Globe-Horn Book Special Citation
   1, 2, 3

> *"My books are about everyday things that are so ordinary that one tends to overlook them. I try to rediscover these things and share them with children."*

Gallob's gift of the camera changed her future. Hoban had never really studied photography, but she found that she had a good sense of light and an eye for interesting pictures. She especially liked to photograph children. Hoban's photos were featured in magazines and included in exhibitions. But Hoban always dreamed of collecting the photographs and presenting them to children.

Her first book, *Shapes and Things,* did just that. It is an exploration of shapes, a celebration of these simple things. Hoban used black-and-white photographs instead of the traditional color illustrations of most children's books. There are no words. The objects alone parade across the pages. A thing is interesting in itself, Hoban seemed to be saying. Children respond well to the book. Even adults sometimes feel as if they are glimpsing the child's world through Hoban's photographs.

> *"I believe certain things happen when the time is right. I also believe that anybody can do anything he or she really wants to."*

The title of Hoban's second book—*Look Again!*—seems to sum up her approach perfectly. Shapes caught her interest. Black-and-

TANA HOBAN CONDUCTED CHILDREN'S PHOTOGRAPHY WORKSHOPS IN FRANCE, TAUGHT PHOTOGRAPHY AT THE UNIVERSITY OF PENNSYLVANIA, AND LECTURED AT MANY OTHER SCHOOLS IN THE UNITED STATES.

white photographs remove the distraction of color. Sometimes Hoban focused on a texture. Her photographs bring out the roughness or smoothness of an object. Wherever she chooses to point her camera, the world became a little more fascinating.

This gifted photographer wrote, designed, illustrated, and published more than one hundred titles. Hoban wanted readers to rediscover everyday things that are ordinary and often overlooked and share them with children.

Tana Hoban lived in Paris, France, until her death in 2006 at the age of eighty-eight.

WHERE TO FIND OUT MORE ABOUT TANA HOBAN

BOOKS

Contemporary Photographers. 3rd ed. Detroit: St. James Press, 1996.

Silvey, Anita, ed. *The Essential Guide to Children's Books and Their Creators.* Boston: Houghton Mifflin Company, 2002.

Something about the Author. Vol. 12. Detroit: Gale, 1991.

WEB SITE

UNIVERSITY OF SOUTHERN MISSISSIPPI DE GRUMMOND COLLECTION
http://www.lib.usm.edu/%7Edegrum/html/research/findaids/hobantan.htm
To read a biographical sketch of and a booklist for Tana Hoban

---

TANA HOBAN APPLIED HER SKILL WITH STILL PHOTOGRAPHY TO MOVING PICTURES. IN 1967, SHE PRODUCED THE FILM *CATSUP*. SHE LATER PRODUCED THE FILMS *WHERE IS IT?* AND *PANDA, PANDA*.

Syd Hoff

Born: September 4, 1912
Died: May 12, 2004

For a short time in college Syd Hoff wanted to be a serious painter. He was inspired by the old masters and other great painters—Rembrandt, Édouard Manet, Leonardo da Vinci. But there was something a little off about his paintings. No matter how hard he tried

to paint seriously, a comic streak kept showing through. His teachers had their doubts, and so did Hoff, for he liked to draw funny things and was very good at it. Today, he is famous for his newspaper comic strips and for books such as *Danny and the Dinosaur*. It seems that Syd Hoff was a pretty funny kid from the start.

Sydney Hoff was born on September 4, 1912, in New York City. His father, Benjamin, was a salesman. His mother,

SYD HOFF'S *DANNY AND THE DINOSAUR* WAS MADE INTO
A FILMSTRIP BY WESTON WOODS STUDIO.

Mary, was very supportive of Syd's early interest in drawing. When he was only three years old, Syd drew a picture of a subway conductor, with his brass-button uniform and conductor's hat. His mother pegged the picture to a wall with a three-inch nail and proclaimed her son to be an artist.

Support for Syd's artistic aspirations came flooding in from other directions, too. When a cartoonist visited his high school, Syd was singled out to join him onstage and draw a cartoon. The cartoonist also proclaimed Syd to be a future artist.

Aside from art class, however, Syd was a miserable student. He dropped out of high school before finishing his last year. Syd still wanted to study art though, so he lied about his age and was accepted to the National Academy of Design in New York City. There he got to know the works of many famous artists and was encouraged by his teachers to take up something else.

At age eighteen, Hoff took that advice. He submitted one of his cartoon drawings to the *New Yorker* magazine, which is famous for

> *"I was born three years after the date of my birth. The family had gone for a ride in the subway and when we came home I drew a picture of the conductor . . . my mother said, 'Sydney is an artist,' and I've been trying to live up to her words ever since."*

CBS BELIEVED THAT SYD HOFF'S HUMOR WOULD WORK WELL ON TELEVISION, AND THEY GAVE HIM HIS OWN TV SERIES CALLED *TALES OF HOFF.*

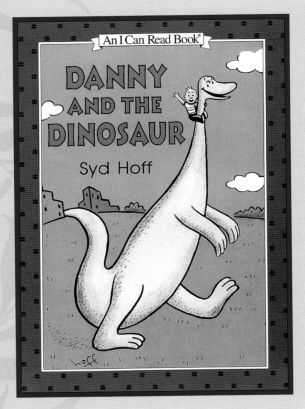

A Selected Bibliography of Hoff's Work

Danny and the Dinosaur Go to Camp (1996)
Happy Birthday, Danny and the Dinosaur! (1995)
Duncan the Dancing Duck (1994)
Bernard on His Own (1993)
Barney's Horse: Story and Pictures (1987)
The Man Who Loved Animals (1982)
Play Ball with Roger the Dodger (1980)
Arthur Gets What He Spills (1979)
Barkley (1975)
The Horse in Harry's Room (1970)
Irving and Me (1967)
Grizzwold (1963)
Albert the Albatross (1961)
Oliver (1960)
Julius (1959)
Sammy the Seal (1959)
Danny and the Dinosaur (1958)

publishing witty cartoons. That cartoon started a long relationship between Hoff and the *New Yorker,* which continued to publish his work. Then, for ten years starting in 1939, his comic strip about a girl named Tuffy appeared in the newspapers and reached millions of readers.

Hoff married Dora Berman in 1937, and the couple had two daughters, Susan and Bonnie. When one of his daughters was undergoing physical therapy, Hoff sketched pictures of a dinosaur and a young boy to cheer her up. The pictures were published as *Danny and the Dinosaur.*

Hoff had tried once before to write a book for children, but it was not much of a hit.

Danny and the Dinosaur, on the other hand, launched a new career for him as a successful children's book author. His drawings are simple pen and ink, sometimes watercolors. They depict the lighthearted world of Danny and

> *"Humor, for some reason, is basically sad. There's some sort of affinity between the sad and the funny that makes it all the funnier."*

his friend the dinosaur, who is on holiday for a day from the museum. Syd Hoff never became a serious painter, but he has entertained many children with his drawings and has become famous for being able to make people laugh.

❧

WHERE TO FIND OUT MORE ABOUT SYD HOFF

BOOKS

De Montreville, Doris, and Donna Hill, eds. *Third Book of Junior Authors.* New York: H. W. Wilson Company, 1972.

Silvey, Anita, ed. *The Essential Guide to Children's Books and Their Creators.* Boston: Houghton Mifflin Company, 2002.

Something about the Author. Vol. 72. Detroit: Gale Research, 1993.

WEB SITE

HARPERCHILDRENS.COM
http://www.harperchildrens.com/catalog/author_xml.asp?authorID=12221
To find out more about Syd Hoff and his books

———

SYD HOFF IS MOST FAMOUS AS A CARTOONIST AND ILLUSTRATOR, BUT HE IS ALSO THE AUTHOR OF MYSTERY STORIES THAT HAVE BEEN PUBLISHED IN *ALFRED HITCHCOCK'S MYSTERY MAGAZINE* AND *ELLERY QUEEN'S MYSTERY MAGAZINE.*

Nonny Hogrogian

Born: May 7, 1932

Nonny Hogrogian has illustrated more than seventy picture books for children. She is especially known for illustrating fairy tales and folktales using rich colors and textures to bring her subjects to life.

Nonny Hogrogian was born in 1932 in New York City. Her family was originally from Armenia, a region in western Asia. She grew up hearing wonderful Armenian folktales from her relatives.

Nonny's father enjoyed painting, and Nonny often dabbled with his painting materials. She began painting when she was three or four. Nonny's grandfather occupied the basement of the Hogrogians' home, and the family library was there, too. Nonny used to sit in her grandfather's big chair and page through books, enchanted by their illustrations. She dreamed of making beautiful pictures herself someday.

HOGRORIAN MADE PAINTED GREETING CARDS FOR STORES IN NEW YORK CITY
WHEN SHE WAS A TEENAGER.

One of Nonny's aunts had studied art in Paris, France. When Nonny was in high school, her aunt taught her painting and charcoal drawing. Nonny also took illustration classes at the Pratt Institute in Brooklyn, New York. Her skills came in handy when she drew illustrations for her high school magazine. She went on to major in art at Hunter College in New York City.

After graduating in 1953, Hogrogian went to work for the William Morrow publishing company. There she helped design book jackets. Meanwhile, she studied with illustrator and artist Antonio Frasconi. He taught her to make woodcuts—illustrations made by carving a

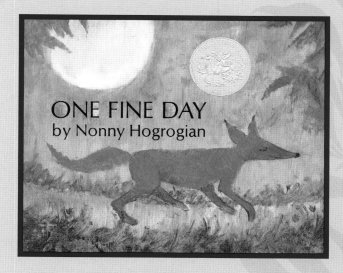

ONE FINE DAY
by Nonny Hogrogian

A Selected Bibliography of Hogrogian's Work

The Tiger of Turkestan (2002)
The Golden Bracelet (Illustrations only, 1997)
Candy Floss (Illustrations only, 1991)
The Cat's Midsummer Jamboree (Illustrations only, 1990)
About Wise Men and Simpletons: Twelve Tales from Grimm (1986)
Root River Run (Illustrations only, 1984)
Country Cat, City Cat (Illustrations only, 1978)
The Contest (1976)
One Fine Day (1971)
The Time-Ago Tales of Jahdu (Illustrations only, 1969)
The Fearsome Inn (Illustrations only, 1967)
Once There Was and Was Not (Illustrations only, 1966)
Always Room for One More (Illustrations only, 1965)
Ghosts Go Haunting (Illustrations only, 1965)
Gaelic Ghosts (Illustrations only, 1963)
King of the Kerry Fair (Illustrations only, 1960)

Hogrogian's Major Literary Awards

1977 Caldecott Honor Book
   The Contest
1972 Caldecott Medal
   One Fine Day
1966 Caldecott Medal
   Always Room for One More

> *"I am always dissatisfied with my work, always left with the feeling that I must try harder the next time."*

design onto a block of wood. Frasconi encouraged the young artist to pursue a career in art.

In 1958, Hogrogian began working at the Thomas Y. Crowell publishing company. There she illustrated her first book—*King of the Kerry Fair*, by Nicolete Meredith—in 1960. Next, Hogrogian took a position as art director at the Holt, Rinehart and Winston publishing company. One of its authors was Leclaire Alger, who wrote under the pen name Sorche Nic Leodhas. Alger wrote Scottish folktales, and Hogrogian was asked to illustrate them. Together they produced *Gaelic Ghosts* in 1963 and *Ghosts Go Haunting* and *Always Room for One More* in 1965.

Hogrogian never forgot the Armenian folktales told to her as a child. In 1971, she used one of those tales in *One Fine Day*, her first illustrated book that she wrote herself. It tells about a fox trying to get its tail back. Another Armenian story inspired Hogrogian's 1976 book *The Contest*, about two robbers who find they're engaged to the same girl.

Hogrogian married poet and author David Kherdian in 1971. As an author-illustrator team, the two went on to produce more than a dozen books together. Many are folktales and poetry collections. Meanwhile, Hogrogian continues to illustrate books written by herself and others.

———

WHEN HOGROGIAN WAS GROWING UP, THREE GENERATIONS OF HER FAMILY LIVED IN A STONE HOUSE IN NEW YORK CITY'S BRONX NEIGHBORHOOD.

> *"Love of work itself was strong in [my] family and whenever there were spare moments someone would start a new project."*

For each book, especially for ethnic folktales, Hogrogian does careful research so her illustrations reflect a region's authentic people, clothing, and customs. She uses many different media in her art, including paint, pen and ink, colored pencils, charcoal, and woodcuts.

Today, Nonny Hogrogian lives in McMinnville, Oregon.

WHERE TO FIND OUT MORE ABOUT NONNY HOGROGIAN

BOOKS

McElmeel, Sharron L. *100 Most Popular Picture Book Authors and Illustrators: Biographical Sketches and Bibliographies.* Englewood, Colo.: Libraries Unlimited, 2000.

Silvey, Anita, ed. *The Essential Guide to Children's Books and Their Creators.* Boston: Houghton Mifflin Company, 2002.

WEB SITES

CHILDREN'S LITERATURE NETWORK
http://www.childrensliteraturenetwork.org/brthpage/05may/5-7hogr.html
For a biography of the artist

NONNY HOGROGIAN
http://www.aaycbook.com/pages/painting_and_drawing/nonny_hogrogian.html
For a biography of Hogrogian

AS A CHILD, HOGROGIAN ENJOYED READING GRIMM'S FAIRY TALES. AS AN ADULT, SHE ILLUSTRATED SEVERAL VOLUMES OF THOSE TALES.

Lee Bennett Hopkins

Born: April 13, 1938

Can a poor student become a successful poet and editor? If you ask Lee Bennett Hopkins, the answer is yes! Hopkins has spent his career bringing the beauty and power of poetry to young people. He has compiled more than eighty anthologies, or collections, of children's poetry. He also writes poems, novels, and nonfiction works of his own.

Lee Bennett Hopkins was born in Scranton, Pennsylvania, in 1938. His family was poor and left for Newark, New Jersey, in 1948 in hopes of finding a better life. Instead, Lee's parents ended up changing jobs frequently, and the family often moved from one apartment to the next.

Lee's parents eventually divorced, and he moved with his mother and siblings into a low-income housing project. "I remember not

HOPKINS'S PARENTS NAMED HIM LEE BENNETT AFTER A POPULAR SINGER FROM THE 1930s.

being interested in anything but survival during this period of my life," Hopkins recalls.

One of Lee's elementary school teachers, Ethel Kite McLaughlin, made a crucial difference in his life. "Mrs. McLaughlin saved me," he says. "She introduced me to two things that had given me direction and hope—the love of reading and the theatre."

Although Lee loved reading, he did poorly in school. Math was especially hard for him. Still, inspired by McLaughlin, he decided to become a schoolteacher. Hopkins worked his way through a teachers' training college but struggled because of his poor academic background.

At last, in 1960, he graduated and landed a teaching job in Fair Lawn, New Jersey. Eventually, Hopkins became a resource teacher—that is, he gathered educational materials for

> *"Children must read and read and read. Reading comes first . . . then comes writing. Poetry should be read every single day of the year, at all times, for all times. Poetry is magical, mystical. I maintain that more can be said or felt in eight or ten or twelve lines than sometimes an entire novel can convey."*

other teachers to use in their classrooms. This was when he discovered that poetry was a great way to help kids learn. He included poems in his resource materials whenever he could.

LEE USED TO HAVE TO STAY HOME FROM SCHOOL TO BABYSIT HIS YOUNGER
BROTHER AND SISTER WHILE HIS MOTHER WENT TO WORK.

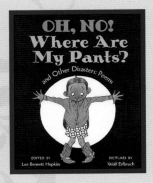

A Selected Bibliography of Hopkins's Work

Got Geography: Poems (2006)

Halloween Howls (2005)

Oh, No! Where Are My Pants? and Other Disasters (2005)

Valentine Hearts: Holiday Poetry (2005)

Alphathoughts: Alphabet Poems (2003)

Hoofbeats, Claws and Rippled Fins: Creature Poems (2002)

Yummy! (2000)

Spectacular Science (1999)

Sports! Sports! Sports! (1999)

Marvelous Math (1997)

Blast Off!: Poems about Space (1995)

Been to Yesterdays: Poems of a Life (1995)

Extra Innings: Baseball Poems (1993)

Flit, Flutter, and Fly (1992)

Ring Out, Wild Bells (1992)

On the Farm (1991)

Voyages (poems by Walt Whitman, 1988)

Crickets and Bullfrogs and Whispers of Thunder (1984)

How Do You Make an Elephant Float? And Other Delicious Riddles (1983)

The Sky Is Full of Song (1983)

Mama and Her Boys (1981)

Elves, Fairies, and Gnomes (1980)

Wonder Wheels (1979)

Merrily Comes Our Harvest In: Poems for Thanksgiving (1978)

Hey-How for Halloween! (1974)

Pass the Poetry, Please! (1972)

Books Are by People (1969)

Hopkins became an editor at a publishing company called Scholastic in 1968. One of his job responsibilities was selecting poems for anthologies. Many of those anthologies center on a certain theme. *The Sky Is Full of Song* presents poetry about the different seasons of the year. Holidays are the theme in *Ring Out, Wild Bells*. *Flit, Flutter, and Fly* offers easy-to-read poems about insects. *Yummy!* is about food.

Hopkins believes that poetry can be used to teach just about any subject. He even published a collection of math-related poems called *Marvelous Math*. He made science fun in his anthology *Spectacular Science*. Hopkins remained with

Scholastic until 1976, when he began working on his own as a full-time writer and anthologist.

It was only natural that Hopkins would eventually write his own poetry. His early work includes a group of autobiographical poems. He has also written three novels for young adults, drawing on experiences from his difficult childhood.

Hopkins now works from his home in Scarborough, New York, overlooking the Hudson River.

> *"There isn't a day that goes by that I'm not reading poetry or working on a poem of my own."*

⚬

WHERE TO FIND OUT MORE ABOUT LEE BENNETT HOPKINS

BOOKS

McElmeel, Sharron L. *100 Most Popular Children's Authors: Biographical Sketches and Bibliographies.* Englewood, Colo.: Libraries Unlimited, 1999.

Silvey, Anita, ed. *The Essential Guide to Children's Books and Their Creators.* Boston: Houghton Mifflin Company, 2002.

WEB SITES

THE CHILDREN'S BOOK COUNCIL
http://www.cbcbooks.org/cbcmagazine/meet/lbhopkins.html
To read an article about the author

HARPERCOLLINS
http://www.harperchildrens.com/authorintro/index.asp?authorid=12232
For a biography about the author

HOPKINS IS THE DONOR OF THE LEE BENNETT HOPKINS POETRY AWARD, PRESENTED BY PENN STATE UNIVERSITY, AND THE LEE BENNETT HOPKINS/INTERNATIONAL READING ASSOCIATION PROMISING POET AWARD.

Deborah Hopkinson

Born: February 4, 1952

Deborah Hopkinson is best known for her historical fiction for children. Using famous moments in history as a backdrop, she weaves exciting tales about children involved in those events.

Deborah Hopkinson was born in Lowell, Massachusetts, in 1952. As a child, she loved reading adventure stories. As a teenager, she enjoyed stories about wars. She always looked forward to summer vacations because then she could stay up late reading.

Hopkinson enrolled in the University of Massachusetts in Amherst, Massachusetts, and majored in English. After graduation in 1973, she moved to Hawaii to attend the University of Hawaii in Honolulu. She received a master's degree in Asian studies in 1978.

Hopkinson made Hawaii her home for nineteen years. She worked as the marketing director for Honolulu's Manoa Valley Theater for

---

HOPKINSON'S KIDS ALWAYS HAD LOTS OF PETS. THEY INCLUDED DOGS, CATS, GEESE, CHICKENS, DOVES, FINCHES, CANARIES, AND PIGEONS.

three years. Then, from 1985 to 1989, she was the development director for the University of Hawaii Foundation. In this position, she was in charge of raising funds for the university. Even after she became an author, she continued to work as a full-time fund-raiser. Meanwhile, she married teacher and artist Andy Thomas. They eventually had two children—Rebekah and Dimitri.

When Rebekah was three years old, Hopkinson found herself reading lots of children's books to her little girl. That's when she began to think about writing for children. As a busy mom who was also working, she figured she only had time to write short stories. For two

A Selected Bibliography of Hopkinson's Work

Sky Boys (2006)

Billy and the Rebel (2005)

From Slave to Soldier (2005)

Apples to Oregon (2004)

A Packet of Seeds (2004)

Girl Wonder (2003)

Shutting Out the Sky: Life in the Tenements of New York, 1880–1924 (2003)

Bluebird Summer (2001)

Fannie in the Kitchen (2001)

Under the Quilt of Night (2000)

A Band of Angels (1998)

Birdie's Lighthouse (1996)

Sweet Clara and the Freedom Quilt (1993)

Pearl Harbor (1991)

Hopkinson's Major Literary Awards

2004 Orbis Pictus Honor Book
   Shutting Out the Sky: Life in the Tenements of New York, 1880–1924

years, she submitted her work to various publishers. Finally, in 1990, her short story "Skate, Kirsten, Skate" was published in *Cricket* magazine.

> "I . . . like to write about girls, because when I was a girl, there weren't many stories about the exciting things that girls can do!"

Hopkinson decided to try writing a book next, and she chose a subject that was close to home. *Pearl Harbor*—her first book, which came out in 1991—was named for a naval base in Hawaii. It tells the story of the Japanese bombing of Pearl Harbor, which led to America's involvement in World War II (1939–1945).

For her next book, Hopkinson ventured into historical fiction. One day, she heard a program on National Public Radio about African American slaves who sewed the patterns of escape routes into handmade quilts. Intrigued by these "freedom quilts," she did extensive research on them. That became the basis for her book *Sweet Clara and the Freedom Quilt*, published in 1993.

At about this time, Hopkinson and her family left Hawaii and moved to Washington State. Still working full-time, she kept writing children's books in her spare moments. Each book is an exciting adventure that profiles an important historical event. *Billy and the Rebel* revolves around events that happened during the Civil War (1861–1865). *Girl Wonder* is based on the life of a girl who became a semiprofessional

---

AFRICAN AMERICAN ARTIST JAMES RANSOME ILLUSTRATED *SWEET CLARA AND THE FREEDOM QUILT*. HE RESEARCHED HIS OWN FAMILY HISTORY IN ORDER TO CREATE THE ART.

baseball player. *Apples to Oregon* tells about the family that introduced fruit trees to Oregon in the 1840s. In her nonfiction book *Shutting Out the Sky: Life in the Tenements of New York, 1880–1924*, Hopkinson describes the lives of immigrants in New York City in the early 1900s.

> *"I think my experience of race was . . . affected by living in Honolulu, America's most multicultural city."*

Besides books, Hopkinson has also written many articles for magazines such as *Cricket*, *Ladybug*, and *Storyworks*. Today, she lives and works in Corvallis, Oregon.

❧

WHERE TO FIND OUT MORE ABOUT DEBORAH HOPKINSON

BOOKS

McElmeel, Sharron L. *100 Most Popular Picture Book Authors and Illustrators: Biographical Sketches and Bibliographies*. Englewood, Colo.: Libraries Unlimited, 2000.

Rockman, Connie C. *Ninth Book of Junior Authors and Illustrators*. New York: H. W. Wilson, 2004.

WEB SITES

DEBORAH HOPKINSON
http://www.deborahhopkinson.com/
To read her biography and link to pages about her work

DOWN HOME BOOKS
http://www.downhomebooks.com/hopkinson.htm
For an interview with the author

WORDS FROM DEBORAH HOPKINSON
http://www.scils.rutgers.edu/~kvander/clara14.html
To read about *Sweet Clara and the Freedom Quilt*

———

HOPKINSON ENJOYS GARDENING, HIKING, SWIMMING, AND READING ABOUT HISTORY.

Polly Horvath

Born: January 30, 1957

Adults often like Polly Horvath's books as much as young readers do. That's just fine with Horvath. She doesn't believe in calling some books "children's books" and other books

"adult books." "When I was a child, my mother used to tell us that anybody can read anything," Horvath says. "I didn't like *Charlotte's Web* as a kid, but I adore it as an adult. This idea of reading within your age slot is bunk. Read what you like."

Polly Horvath was born on January 30, 1957, in Kalamazoo, Michigan. Her father, John, was a teacher. Her mother, Betty, was a writer. When Polly was a girl, her parents encouraged her interest

HORVATH SAYS HER WRITING HAS BEEN INFLUENCED BY THE WORK OF CHARLES DICKENS AND MARK TWAIN.

in reading. By the time she was nine, Polly had begun writing her first stories. She continued to write all through her childhood and teen years.

When she turned eighteen, Horvath decided to pursue another talent. She began studying dance. She attended the Martha Graham School of Contemporary Dance in New York and the Canadian College of Dance in Toronto, Ontario. She planned to pursue a career as a dance teacher. In Canada, she met her husband, Arnold Keller, an English professor. Horvath has lived in Canada since 1975.

Horvath continued to write stories and send them to publishers. Although she was

A Selected Bibliography of Horvath's Work

Vacation (2005)
Pepins and Their Problems (2004)
The Canning Season (2002)
Everything on a Waffle (2001)
The Trolls (1999)
When the Circus Came to Town (1996)
The Happy Yellow Car (1994)
No More Cornflakes (1990)
An Occasional Cow (1989)

Horvath's Major Literary Awards

2003 National Book Award
   The Canning Season

2002 Newbery Honor Book
2001 Boston Globe-Horn Book Fiction and Poetry Honor Book
   Everything on a Waffle

1999 Boston Globe-Horn Book Fiction Honor Book
   The Trolls

> *"It's not the natural disasters you have to fear. It's the ones inside you, waiting to happen."*

sometimes discouraged by rejections, she did not give up.

Finally, in 1989, she published her first book, *An Occasional Cow.* The book is about a ten-year-old girl named Imogene who goes to stay with cousins in Iowa for one summer. The following year, Horvath published her second book, *No More Cornflakes.* In *No More Cornflakes,* a ten-year-old girl named Hortense has to survive big changes in her family, including her mother expecting a baby.

Horvath's next book was set during the hard times of the Great Depression of the 1930s. In *The Happy Yellow Car,* Betty Grunt is shocked when her father comes home with a fancy yellow car, which he bought with money the family had saved for Betty's college education.

Horvath's 1999 book, *The Trolls,* shows her affection for her adopted country, Canada. Aunt Sally from Canada comes to visit her nieces and nephews who live in Ohio. At first, the children don't know what to make of Aunt Sally, but she eventually wins them over.

Horvath's book *Everything on a Waffle* is her first to be based in Canada. Set in a town on the Pacific coast of Canada, the book is about a girl named Primrose Squarp. Although everyone tells Primrose

---

NICKELODEON IS AT WORK ON A PRODUCTION OF *THE TROLLS.*

that her parents have been lost at sea, Primrose refuses to believe it. One of the book's themes is the way people can deal with loss without losing hope.

Polly Horvath lives with her husband and two daughters in Metchosin, British Columbia. She is at work on a new novel for children.

> *"I don't feel I approach a new book. I always feel a new book approaches me. I just sit down and write."*

WHERE TO FIND OUT MORE ABOUT POLLY HORVATH

BOOKS

Rockman, Connie C., ed. *The Ninth Book of Junior Authors and Illustrators.* New York: H. W. Wilson Company, 2004.

Silvey, Anita, ed. *The Essential Guide to Children's Books and Their Creators.* Boston: Houghton Mifflin Company, 2002.

WEB SITES

KIDSREADS.COM
http://www.kidsreads.com/reviews/0374322368.asp
To read a synopsis of Polly Horvath's *Everything on a Waffle*

POLLY HORVATH HOME PAGE
http://www.pollyhorvath.com/
For biographical information and a list of her books

HORVATH IS ONLY THE SECOND CANADIAN RESIDENT TO HAVE EARNED A NEWBERY HONOR.

James Howe

Born: August 2, 1946

umor is an important part of James Howe's books. "Humor is the most precious gift I can give to my reader," Howe has said. He has written more than fifty books for children and young people. He has written picture books, novels, and screenplays for movies and television shows. His most popular books include the Bunnicula series, the Sebastian Barth series, and the Pinky and Rex series.

James Howe was born on August 2, 1946, in Oneida, New York. As a young boy, he enjoyed making up stories with his friends. His family also stimulated his imagination and interest in words and

BUNNICULA: A RABBIT-TALE OF MYSTERY, THE STORY OF
A PET RABBIT THAT IS THOUGHT TO ACT LIKE A VAMPIRE, WAS
ADAPTED INTO AN ANIMATED TELEVISION MOVIE THAT AIRED IN **1982.**

writing. "Words played an important part in my growing up," Howe says. "Not only the written word, but words that flew through the air—jokes, riddles, puns. My family was always playing with words."

James found writing to be fun and entertaining. He wrote and performed in his first play when he was seven years old. Later, he wrote short stories and humor columns for his high school newspaper. He even published his own newspaper that he called the *Gory Gazette*.

When Howe entered college at Boston University, he wanted to become an actor rather than a writer. "As much as I loved writing plays, I loved performing in them even more," Howe notes. He received a fine arts degree in 1968 and worked as a social worker for a short time. He then pursued his acting career and appeared in television commercials. Howe also directed several plays and worked as an agent for other writers.

A few years later Howe went to graduate school and took a playwriting class, which reminded him of his love for writing. Howe's wife, Deborah, encouraged him to write a children's book about a rabbit

"Most of my stories are humorous, but they almost always have something serious going on in them as well. That's because I can no more separate my serious concerns about the world from my cockeyed way of seeing it than I can keep apart my personal and professional selves."

IN HIS NONFICTION BOOK *THE HOSPITAL BOOK,* HOWE DESCRIBES MEDICAL PROCEDURES FROM A CHILD'S POINT OF VIEW. THIS BOOK HELPS CHILDREN UNDERSTAND WHAT IT IS LIKE TO BE IN A HOSPITAL.

A Selected Bibliography of Howe's Work

Bunnicula Meets Edgar Allan Crow (2006)

Vampire Bunny (2005)

Howie Monroe and the Doghouse of Doom (2002)

Horace and Morris Join the Chorus (But What about Dolores?) (2001)

Horace and Morris But Mostly Dolores (1999)

Harold & Chester in Scared Silly: A Halloween Treat (1998)

There's a Dragon in My Sleeping Bag (1994)

Rabbit-Cadabra! (1993)

Return to Howliday Inn (1992)

Harold & Chester in Creepy Crawly Birthday (1991)

Eat Your Poison, Dear (1990)

There's a Monster under My Bed (1990)

Harold & Chester in the Fright before Christmas (1988)

Nighty-Nightmare (1987)

When You Go to Kindergarten (1986)

Howliday Inn (1986)

What Eric Knew: A Sebastian Barth Mystery (1985)

The Day the Teacher Went Bananas (1984)

The Celery Stalks at Midnight (1983)

The Hospital Book (1981)

Bunnicula: A Rabbit-Tale of Mystery (With Deborah Howe, 1979)

Howe's Major Literary Award

1981 Boston Globe–Horn Book Nonfiction Honor Book
  The Hospital Book

character that he had created several years earlier.

At the same time, Deborah became sick with cancer. As a way to cope with the illness, James and Deborah worked together on this book. Deborah died of cancer in 1978, but the book, *Bunnicula: A Rabbit-Tale of Mystery,* was published in 1979. Howe also published one other book that he cowrote with Deborah. He went on to write many more *Bunnicula* books and other book series for children.

Howe's books are full of humor, but they also include serious issues. He believes that it is important to be open and honest when writing for young people. "It's the writer's privilege and responsibility to give children a world they can enter, recognize, at times be frightened of, but which ultimately, they can master and control," Howe says.

Howe lives in Hastings-on-Hudson, New York, with his second wife and their daughter. He continues to write both fiction and nonfiction books for children and young people.

> *"I don't believe I was born to write. But the creative itch has been with me for as long as I can remember. And it has always been strong enough that it demanded to be scratched."*

❧

WHERE TO FIND OUT MORE ABOUT JAMES HOWE

BOOKS

Holtze, Sally Holmes, ed. *Sixth Book of Junior Authors & Illustrators.* New York: H. W. Wilson Company, 1989.

Howe, James. *Playing with Words.* Katonah, N.Y.: Owen, 1994.

Silvey, Anita, ed. *The Essential Guide to Children's Books and Their Creators.* Boston: Houghton Mifflin Company, 2002.

WEB SITE

SCHOLASTIC AUTHORS AND BOOKS
http://books.scholastic.com/teachers/authorsandbooks/authorstudies/authorhome.jsp? authorID=1832&collateralID=10322&displayName=Biography
To read a biography of James Howe and to explore his books

SOME OF HOWE'S WORKS HAVE BEEN TRANSLATED INTO FRENCH, GERMAN, SWEDISH, DANISH, ITALIAN, JAPANESE, SPANISH, AND DUTCH.

Langston Hughes

Born: February 1, 1902
Died: May 22, 1967

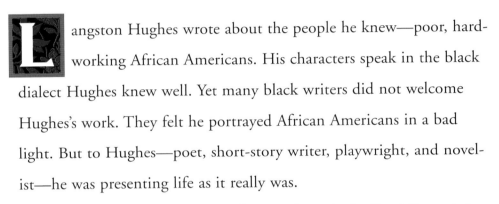

Langston Hughes wrote about the people he knew—poor, hard-working African Americans. His characters speak in the black dialect Hughes knew well. Yet many black writers did not welcome Hughes's work. They felt he portrayed African Americans in a bad light. But to Hughes—poet, short-story writer, playwright, and novelist—he was presenting life as it really was.

James Mercer Langston Hughes was born in Joplin, Missouri, in 1902. His ancestors included African American, Native American, and white people, including slave traders and owners. Langston's mother was a bright, creative, college-educated woman. His father had studied law, but African Americans were not allowed to work as lawyers in the United States. When Langston was a child, his father moved to Mexico, where he became a successful attorney.

OTHER ARTISTS WHO TOOK PART IN THE HARLEM RENAISSANCE MOVEMENT WERE WRITERS COUNTEE CULLEN AND ZORA NEALE HURSTON, MUSICIANS LOUIS ARMSTRONG AND BILLIE HOLIDAY, AND ACTOR PAUL ROBESON.

Langston spent much of his childhood with his grandmother, Mary Leary Langston, in Lawrence, Kansas. Through her, he learned to love books and to value education. She was a great storyteller, too—full of inspiring stories about African Americans' struggles for freedom.

In 1915, Langston and his mother moved to Lincoln, Illinois, where he was named Class Poet at his grammar school. Another move took them to Cleveland, Ohio. Hughes attended New York City's Columbia University for a year and then graduated from Lincoln University in Pennsylvania.

Hughes published his first poetry collection, *The Weary Blues*, in 1926. *Fine Clothes to*

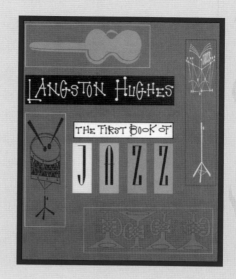

A Selected Bibliography of Hughes's Work

Black Misery (1969)
Don't You Turn Back (1969)
The Panther and the Lash (1967)
Fight for Freedom: The Story of the NAACP (1962)
Ask Your Mama: 12 Moods for Jazz (1961)
The First Book of Africa (1960)
Simple Stakes a Claim (1957)
The First Book of Jazz (1955)
Montage of a Dream Deferred (1951)
Simple Speaks His Mind (1950)
Fields of Wonder (1947)
Lament for Dark Peoples and Other Poems (1944)
Shakespeare in Harlem (1942)
Mulatto (1935)
The Ways of White Folks (1934)
The Dream Keeper and Other Poems (1932)
The Negro Mother and Other Dramatic Recitations (1931)
Not without Laughter (1930)
Fine Clothes to the Jew (1927)
The Weary Blues (1926)

> *"I didn't know the upper-class Negroes well enough to write much about them. I knew only the people I had grown up with, and they weren't people whose shoes were always shined, who had been to Harvard, or who had heard of Bach. But they seemed to me good people, too."*

the Jew followed in 1927. Many white critics praised Hughes's writing, but black reviewers were vicious. They called his work trash, low-rate, and a disgrace. During this time, Hughes became an important figure in the Harlem Renaissance—a literary, artistic, and intellectual movement centered in the Harlem district of New York City. African American writers, artists, and musicians blossomed, and they approached their arts from a black point of view, kindling a new cultural identity.

In the early 1930s, Hughes traveled all over the world. In Russia, he wrote the first three of his first short stories to be published. Back in the United States, he started writing plays and soon founded several theater companies. In 1942, Hughes began writing a column for the black-owned newspaper the *Chicago Defender*. He created a character called Jesse B. Semple (later changed to Simple). Simple moves from the rural South to an industrial city in the North to find work. But he only finds new forms of racism, and he makes humorous, biting comments about it. Hughes's tales about Simple were later published as short-story collections.

———

HUGHES WAS THE FIRST AFRICAN AMERICAN TO SUPPORT HIMSELF COMPLETELY BY WRITING. AS A YOUNG MAN, HE WORKED AS A TRUCK FARMER, A COOK ON SHIPS, A WAITER, AND A DOORMAN IN A NIGHTCLUB IN PARIS, FRANCE.

Hughes wrote most of his books for young people in the 1950s. They are clear explanations of subjects such as Africa, the civil rights movement, and jazz. The racial unrest of the 1960s brought out Hughes's anger about racial segregation. These feelings are shown in *Ask Your Mama: 12 Moods for Jazz*, a collection of poetry to be read along with jazz music. More poems of protest appear in *The Panther and the Lash*. It was published shortly after Hughes died of heart problems in 1967.

> *"Most people are generally good, in every race and in every country where I have been."*

Today, Hughes is still honored as a writer who captured the true sounds and rhythms of African American life.

WHERE TO FIND OUT MORE ABOUT LANGSTON HUGHES

BOOKS

Hughes, Langston. *The Big Sea: An Autobiography.* New York: Hill and Wang, 1993.

Silvey, Anita, ed. *The Essential Guide to Children's Books and Their Creators.* Boston: Houghton Mifflin Company, 2002.

WEB SITE

JOURNEYS AND CROSSING—LIBRARY OF CONGRESS
http://www.loc.gov/rr/program/journey/hughes.html
To read a transcript, view a Webcast, and link to other sites about Langston Hughes

IN THE 1920S, HUGHES TRAVELED THROUGH THE SOUTH WITH FELLOW WRITER ZORA NEALE HURSTON. THEY COLLECTED INFORMATION ABOUT SOUTHERN BLACK FOLKLORE AND FOLK TRADITIONS.

Johanna Hurwitz

Born: October 9, 1937

Johanna Hurwitz has written more than fifty books for young readers. Even as a child, books were an important part of her life. Johanna Hurwitz was born in New York City on October 9, 1937. Her father, Nelson, was a journalist and bookseller. Her mother, Tillie, was a library assistant. The walls of the family's New York apart-

ment were lined with books. Johanna herself became interested in books at an early age. She applied for a public library card as soon as she was old enough. Before she was ten, she had decided that she would become a professional writer.

While in high school, Johanna began working at the New York Public Library. She graduated from Queens College in 1958, and received a master's degree in library science

---

JOHANNA HURWITZ'S FATHER ONCE RAN A USED BOOKSTORE IN NEW YORK CITY.

from Columbia University in 1959. After graduation, she began working as a full-time children's librarian. She married Uri Hurwitz in 1962. The couple have two children, Nomi and Benjamin.

Hurwitz began writing stories when she was a girl. However, she did not publish her first book until 1976. It was called *Busybody Nora,* and it was based on her own experiences raising her two children. *Busybody Nora* is the story of a curious seven-year-old, a character inspired by Hurwitz's daughter, Nomi. Nora's little brother, Teddy, is based on Hurwitz's son, Benjamin.

Nora also appears in several other Hurwitz books, includ-

A Selected Bibliography of Hurwitz's Work

Unsigned Valentine: And Other Events in the Life of Emma Meade (2006)
Fourth Grade Fuss (2004)
Dear Emma (2002)
Oh No, Noah! (2002)
Ethan at Home (2001)
Superduper Teddy (2001)
Pee Wee's Tale (2000)
Aldo Ice Cream (1999)
Aldo Peanut Butter (1999)
The Just Desserts Club (1999)
A Dream Come True (1998)
Ever-Clever Elisa (1997)
Helen Keller: Courage in the Dark (1997)
The Down & Up Fall (1996)
Elisa in the Middle (1995)
A Word to the Wise: And Other Proverbs (1994)
Leonard Bernstein: A Passion for Music (1993)
Roz and Ozzie (1992)
New Neighbors for Nora (1991)
Nora and Mrs. Mind-Your-Own Business (1991)
Tough-Luck Karen (1991)
Astrid Lindgren: Storyteller to the World (1989)
Hurray for Ali Baba Bernstein (1989)
Anne Frank: Life in Hiding (1988)
Class Clown (1987)
Russell Sprouts (1987)
A Yellow Blue Jay (1987)
Hurricane Elaine (1986)
The Adventures of Ali Baba Bernstein (1985)
The Hot & Cold Summer (1985)
The Rabbi's Girls (1982)
Tough-Luck Karen (1982)
Baseball Fever (1981)
Aldo Applesauce (1979)
The Law of Gravity: A Story (1978)
Busybody Nora (1976)

ing *Nora and Mrs. Mind-Your-Own-Business* and *New Neighbors for Nora.* Teddy is the main character in a book called *Superduper Teddy.* "It seems as if all my fiction has grown out of real experiences," Hurwitz once explained. "It took me many years to realize that my everyday life contained the substance for the books I fantasized I would write."

Her children's love of baseball helped inspire Hurwitz's book *Baseball Fever.* A summer vacation in Vermont inspired *Yellow Blue Jay.* Stories of her mother's childhood were the basis for her book *The Rabbi's Girls.*

> "I write for children because I am especially interested in that period of life. There is an intensity and seriousness about childhood that fascinates me."

Hurwitz has invented several fictional families that make repeat appearances in her books. For example, the Sossi family is featured in *Aldo Ice Cream.* In that book, fourth-grader Aldo Sossi sets out to sample every flavor at the local ice cream parlor. In *Aldo Peanut Butter,* he raises puppies named Peanut and Butter. Aldo's thirteen-year-old sister Karen is the main character in *Tough-Luck Karen.* Another sister is featured in *Hurricane Elaine.*

Hurwitz has also written several books about real people. She is the author of four biographies of important historical figures. Her book *Anne Frank: Life in Hiding* tells the story of the now-famous Jewish girl who lived in hiding during World War II (1939–1945). *Astrid Lindgren:*

WHEN SHE WAS A GIRL, JOHANNA HURWITZ LIVED SO CLOSE TO YANKEE STADIUM IN NEW YORK THAT SHE COULD HEAR BASEBALL FANS CHEERING FROM HER HOUSE.

Storyteller to the World is about the creator of the Pippi Longstocking books. *Leonard Bernstein: A Passion for Music* introduces young readers to the American conductor and composer. *Helen Keller: Courage in the Dark* is about the famous blind and deaf American author.

Hurwitz lives in Great Neck, New York. She continues to be inspired to write books for children.

"If upon completion of my book, the reader is eager to read another (by me or by someone else too), then I know I have been successful."

❧

WHERE TO FIND OUT MORE ABOUT JOHANNA HURWITZ

BOOKS

Kovacs, Deborah, and James Preller. *Meet the Authors and Illustrators: 60 Creators of Favorite Children's Books Talk about Their Work.* Vol. 2. New York: Scholastic, 1993.

McElmeel, Sharron L. *100 Most Popular Children's Authors: Biographical Sketches and Bibliographies.* Englewood, Colo.: Libraries Unlimited, 1999.

Silvey, Anita, ed. *Children's Books and Their Authors.* Boston: Houghton Mifflin, 1995.

WEB SITES

EDUCATIONAL PAPERBACK ASSOCIATION
http://edupaperback.org/showauth2.cfm?authid=135
To read an autobiographical sketch and booklist for Johanna Hurwitz

HARPERCOLLINS CHILDREN'S BOOKS: JOHANNA HURWITZ
http://www.harperchildrens.com/authorintro/index.asp?authorid=14706
To read a biography of Johanna Hurwitz, to read about her life in her own words, and to explore her many books

———

HURWITZ OWNS TWO CATS, SINBAD AND SELENA.

Pat Hutchins

Born: June 18, 1942

Pat Hutchins got many of the ideas for her books from watching her own children. She also writes about experiences that she remembers from her own childhood. Hutchins writes and illustrates picture books. Her best-known books include *The Very Worst Monster, The Wind Blew, Where's the Baby?* and *Tidy Titch.* Hutchins has also written several fiction books for young people, which her husband, Laurence Hutchins, illustrated.

She was born Patricia Goundry on June 18, 1942, in Yorkshire, England. She grew up the sixth of seven children. Pat loved to wander around the countryside with her friends. She liked to read, draw, and often carried her sketch pad with her.

———

HUTCHINS WROTE *HAPPY BIRTHDAY, SAM* FOR HER OWN SON SAM.

"I was brought up in a small village in Yorkshire. . . . As I loved drawing, I would wander round the country-side with my drawing book under my arm and my pet crow on my shoulder (he was too lazy to fly) and, while he searched for grubs, I sketched. Books were my other love, so it was inevitable that I would go to art school and study illustration."

Pat's mother often took care of injured animals. One of the animals that Pat's mother nursed back to health was a crow. Pat named the crow Sooty. Pat let the crow sit on her shoulder. When she walked in the woods, Sooty went with her!

When she was sixteen years old, Pat received a scholarship to attend a local art school. She studied there for three years. She then went on to study illustration at Leeds College of Art in England.

After college, she went to London to find a job and was hired by an advertising agency. She met and married Laurence Hutchins while working at the agency. Just days after they were married, he was transferred to the agency's office in New York City.

Pat Hutchins and her husband lived in a small apartment in New York City. She did not have much to do and decided

"I feel that ultimately you write to satisfy yourself and hope that your readers will be satisfied with your offering, too."

TIDY TITCH IS BASED ON HUTCHINS'S SONS, SAM AND MORGAN.

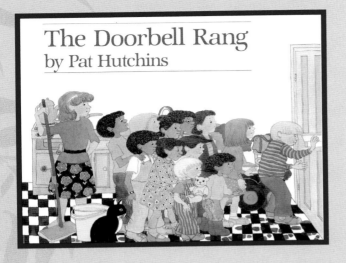

The Doorbell Rang
by Pat Hutchins

A Selected Bibliography of Hutchins's Work

Barn Dance (2007)

Bumpety Bump (2006)

Don't Get Lost (2004)

Only One of Me (2003)

We're Going on a Picnic! (2001)

Ten Red Apples (2000)

Tidy Titch (1999)

It's My Birthday! (1998)

Shrinking Mouse (1997)

Clocks and More Clocks (1994)

Little Pink Pig (1994)

My Best Friend (1993)

Where's the Baby? (1988)

The Doorbell Rang (1986)

The Very Worst Monster (1985)

King Henry's Palace (1983)

One-Eyed Jake (1979)

The Best Train Set Ever (1978)

Happy Birthday, Sam (1978)

The Wind Blew (1974)

Good Night, Owl! (1972)

Changes, Changes (1971)

Rosie's Walk (1967)

Hutchins's Major Literary Awards

1974 Kate Greenaway Medal
  The Wind Blew

1968 Boston Globe–Horn Book Picture Book Honor Book
  Rosie's Walk

to spend her time writing and illustrating a children's book.

In 1968, after eighteen months, the couple moved back to London. That year her first son was born and her first book, *Rosie's Walk,* was published. Her second son was born five years later. Since then, Pat Hutchins has written and illustrated more than thirty books for children.

Hutchins enjoys writing for children. "I think one can get quite complicated ideas across to small children as long as they are presented in

"To me, the most important thing about a children's picture book is that it should be logical."

a simple, satisfying way," Hutchins notes. She includes humor in her books and writes about things from the lives of children.

Hutchins lives in a part of London called Hampstead with her husband. She continues to write and illustrate books for children and young people.

✿

WHERE TO FIND OUT MORE ABOUT PAT HUTCHINS

BOOKS

Collier, Laurie, and Joyce Nakamura, eds. *Major Authors and Illustrators for Children and Young Adults.* Detroit: Gale Research, 1993.

Kovacs, Deborah, and James Preller. *Meet the Authors and Illustrators: 60 Creators of Favorite Children's Books Talk about Their Work.* Vol. 1. New York: Scholastic, 1991.

McElmeel, Sharron L. *100 Most Popular Children's Authors: Biographical Sketches and Bibliographies.* Englewood, Colo.: Libraries Unlimited, 1999.

Silvey, Anita, ed. *The Essential Guide to Children's Books and Their Creators.* Boston: Houghton Mifflin Company, 2002.

WEB SITES
CAROL HURST CHILDREN'S LITERATURE SITE
http://www.carolhurst.com/authors/hutchins.html
For a brief biographical sketch of Pat Hutchins and synopses of several of her books

TITCH BY PAT HUTCHINS
http://www.titch.net
To read about Hutchins's books, to see photgraphs of the author, and find out answers to questions frequently asked of Hutchins

AS A YOUNG CHILD, HUTCHINS LIVED IN AN ARMY TRAINING CAMP. SHE PLAYED IN THE FIELDS WHERE THE SOLDIERS DID THEIR TRAINING.

Trina Schart Hyman

Born: April 8, 1939
Died: November 19, 2004

I f you have ever seen pictures of Saint George battling a dragon to save the English kingdom or beautiful pictures of Sleeping Beauty, you may have seen the work of Trina Schart Hyman. Her illustrations have brought to life more than a hundred children's stories. She gave

children images of knights battling evil in a halo of light and of monsters that are truly horrible to look upon.

The creator of these fantastic visions was born in Philadelphia, Pennsylvania, on April 8, 1939, the daughter of Albert Schart, a salesman, and Margaret Doris Schart. Trina Hyman said that the secret of turning a fictional character into a memorable picture is a fascination with people—their characters, expressions,

TRINA SCHART HYMAN'S VIVID ILLUSTRATIONS LEND THEMSELVES TO FILM ADAPTATIONS. *DRAGON STEW, TIGHT TIMES,* AND *LITTLE RED RIDING HOOD* HAVE ALL BEEN MADE INTO FILMSTRIPS OR TELEVISION SPECIALS.

and behaviors. She has tried to discover what makes a knight dashing, a maiden beautiful, or a monster frightening. Then she made it plain to the reader through her drawings and paintings. Her gift for art was enhanced by training at the Philadelphia Museum College of Art and the Boston Museum of Fine Arts School.

In 1959, she married Harris Hyman. The couple has one daughter, Katrin. In 1960, Hyman was admitted to the Swedish State Art School. She

A Selected Bibliography of Hyman's Work

Little Women, or, Meg, Jo, Beth, and Amy (Illustrations only, 2002)

Children of the Dragon: Selected Tales from Vietnam (Illustrations only, 2001)

The Alphabet Game (2000)

A Child's Calendar (Illustrations only, 1999)

A Smile So Big (Illustrations only, 1998)

Comus (Illustrations only, 1996)

Winter Poems (Illustrations only, 1994)

The Fortune-Tellers (Illustrations only, 1992)

Ghost Eye (Illustrations only, 1992)

Hershel and the Hanukkah Goblins (Illustrations only, 1989)

A Child's Christmas in Wales (Illustrations only, 1985)

Saint George and the Dragon: A Golden Legend (Illustrations only, 1984)

Little Red Riding Hood (1983)

Tight Times (Illustrations only, 1979)

On to Widecombe Fair (Illustrations only, 1978)

King Stork (Illustrations only, 1973)

Dragon Stew (Illustrations only, 1969)

All in Free but Janey (Illustrations only, 1968)

Hyman's Major Literary Awards

2000 Caldecott Honor Book
A Child's Calendar

1993 Boston Globe-Horn Book Picture Book Award
The Fortune-Tellers

1990 Caldecott Honor Book
Hershel and the Hanukkah Goblins

1985 Caldecott Medal
St. George and the Dragon: A Golden Legend

1984 Caldecott Honor Book
Little Red Riding Hood

1978 Boston Globe-Horn Book Picture Book Honor Book
On to Widecombe Fair

1976 Boston Globe-Horn Book Nonfiction Honor Book
Will You Sign Here, John Hancock?

1973 Boston Globe-Horn Book Picture Book Award
King Stork

1968 Boston Globe-Horn Book Picture Book Honor Book
All in Free but Janey

> "One of the nicest things about being an artist is the ability to see things a little differently, . . . more carefully, . . . more imaginatively, than most other people do . . . to see the possibilities in things, to see the magic, . . . to see what it is that makes that thing inherently itself."

struggled to master Swedish and landed her first job as an illustrator. When she returned to the United States, she was offered an illustrating job by one of her friends who worked at Little, Brown Publishing. It was just the first of many such projects. Her illustrations proved to be popular with authors and readers. She had a knack for capturing a book's atmosphere. Her illustrations give the characters real personalities, no matter how minor their role in the story.

In 1972, Hyman took a job as art director of *Cricket* magazine. Aside from designing covers and laying out the interiors, she came into contact with many writers and illustrators. This brought her many offers to illustrate books. She is perhaps most famous for her illustrations of classic children's tales. She illustrated stories by the Brothers Grimm, Charles

> "The focus of my illustrations—largely because of the kinds of stories I choose to illustrate—is almost always on human beings. People—and this includes monsters and other fantastic creatures—are endlessly fascinating to me as subject matter."

TRINA SCHART HYMAN RECEIVED HER FIRST ILLUSTRATING JOB WHILE STUDYING IN SWEDEN. SHE SAID THAT IT TOOK HER NEARLY AS LONG TO READ THE BOOK IN SWEDISH AS IT DID TO DO THE ILLUSTRATIONS.

Dickens, Mark Twain, and Hans Christian Andersen. Her depiction of the medieval world, with its knights, castles, monks, village girls, and princes has earned much attention. Her painting captures the finery of a noble's robes and the wretchedness of an old hag. In her work, the world of fantasy and magic seems real and fantastic at the same time. Hyman had a romantic vision, more stunning than reality, and it captures the wonder of the world of the imagination and of times long forgotten. Through Trina Schart Hyman's vision, fantastic stories come to life, giving children images that might well stay with them for a lifetime.

❧

WHERE TO FIND OUT MORE ABOUT TRINA SCHART HYMAN

BOOKS

Hyman, Trina Schart. *Self Portrait: Trina Schart Hyman.*
Reading, Mass.: Addison-Wesley, 1981.

Kovacs, Deborah, and James Preller. *Meet the Authors and Illustrators: 60 Creators of Favorite Children's Books Talk about Their Work.* Vol. 1. New York: Scholastic, 1991.

WEB SITES

UNIVERSITY OF SOUTHERN MISSISSIPPI DE GRUMMOND COLLECTION
http://www.lib.usm.edu/%7Edegrum/html/research/findaids/hyman.htm
To read a biographical sketch and booklist for Trina Schart Hyman

WOMEN CHILDREN'S BOOK ILLUSTRATORS
http://www.ortakales.com/illustrators/Hyman.html
To read a biographical sketch of Trina Schart Hyman, a summary
of her awards, and synopses of some of her books

BESIDES PAINTING MEDIEVAL AND FAIRY-TALE CHARACTERS, TRINA SCHART HYMAN
DEPICTED LIFE IN PLACES AS FAR AWAY AS WEST AFRICA AND SOUTHEAST ASIA.

Rachel Isadora

Born: 1953

As a young girl, dancing was an important part of Rachel Isadora's life. She spent many years training to be a dancer. Many of her books for children are about dancing and the arts. Isadora has written and illustrated more than forty books for children. Her best-known books include *Ben's Trumpet, My Ballet Diary, Isadora Dances,* and *Sophie Skates.*

Rachel Isadora was born in 1953, in New York City. She began taking dance lessons when she was a toddler after she wandered into her older sister's dance class. She took many different dance lessons and became a very good dancer. When Rachel was eleven years old,

---

ISADORA IS BEST KNOWN FOR HER BOOK *BEN'S TRUMPET,*
WHICH WAS A **1980** CALDECOTT HONOR BOOK.

she performed with a professional ballet company. She also received a scholarship to attend a ballet school.

Rachel was very shy as a young girl. She would not practice her dances when people could see her. She would observe in her dance class. Then she would rehearse by herself until she learned the dance moves. She let people watch her dance only after she had learned the steps.

> *"Work like this is a dancer's fantasy. Because ballet is so demanding, dancers' stage careers are short. They can only dream of going on and on forever. With art, I can go on and on, and for me it's the only work that compares in intensity and joy."*

Rachel also felt a great deal of pressure as a dancer. Then she discovered that she liked to draw. She used her drawing as a way to release the pressure. "To escape it, I drew—so that became my fantasy world," she noted. "I could express my thoughts in it, I could even express my anger. I couldn't do that as a dancer." She did not show her drawings to anyone. She did not even show the drawings to her parents.

When Rachel was seventeen years old, she was offered a chance to dance with a professional ballet company in New York. But she felt too much pressure and did not do it. She did not dance for several

ISADORA AND HER HUSBAND, JAMES TURNER, HAVE ONE DAUGHTER, GILLIAN.

A Selected Bibliography of Isadora's Work

Yo, Jo! (2007)

What a Family (2005)

In the Beginning (2003)

On Your Toes: A Ballet ABC (2003)

Bring On That Beat (2002)

Nick Plays Baseball (2001)

123 Pop! (2000)

Sophie Skates (1999)

Isadora Dances (1998)

My Ballet Diary (1995)

At the Crossroads (1994)

Prayers, Praises, and Thanksgivings (Illustrations only, 1992)

Swan Lake (1991)

The Little Match Girl (Illustrations only, 1987)

Opening Night (1984)

A Little Interlude (Illustrations only, 1980)

Ben's Trumpet (1979)

Backstage (1978)

Max (1976)

Isadora's Major Literary Awards

1979 Boston Globe–Horn Book Picture Book Honor Book
1980 Caldecott Honor Book
   Ben's Trumpet

years. She then had a chance to dance for a ballet company in Boston. But she injured her foot and was no longer able to dance. She needed to find a way to earn money.

Isadora decided to look for a job as an illustrator. She showed her collection of drawings to publishers in New York. It did not take long for her to find work. She was asked to work on a children's book. The book, *Max,* was published in 1976. She has written and illustrated many other books for children during her career.

> *"I see the way a child sees. So I decided, I'll just draw it the way I see it, and the kids will see it their way."*

Isadora continues to write for children and young people. She lives in New York with her family.

⚬

WHERE TO FIND OUT MORE ABOUT RACHEL ISADORA

BOOKS

Holtze, Sally Holmes, ed. *Fifth Book of Junior Authors & Illustrators.*
New York: H. W. Wilson Company, 1983.

Silvey, Anita, ed. *The Essential Guide to Children's Books and Their Creators.*
Boston: Houghton Mifflin Company, 2002.

WEB SITE
HARPER COLLINS
http://www.harpercollinschildrens.com/HarperChildrens/Kids/AuthorsAndIllustrators/
ContributorDetail.aspx?CId=17066
To read a biographical sketch of Rachel Isadora

ISADORA AND HER FIRST HUSBAND, ROBERT MAIORANO, WORKED TOGETHER ON SEVERAL BOOKS. TWO OF THEM ARE *BACKSTAGE* AND *A LITTLE INTERLUDE.*

Brian Jacques

Born: June 15, 1939

Authors of great children's books sometimes write a story for a specific child or group of children, never imagining or intending that it will be published. This happened with *Alice in Wonderland* and *The Hobbit*, for example. It was also the case with Brian Jacques and his book *Redwall*, the first of what would become an enormously popular series.

Brian Jacques was born in Liverpool, England, on June 15, 1939. Like many people in this port city, Brian's family was originally from County Cork in Ireland. Growing up near the Liverpool docks, Brian imagined himself heading off to sea for many adventures.

Growing up, Brian's imagination was fueled by the adventure books he loved reading. Books such as *Robinson Crusoe, Treasure Island,* and *A Wind in the Willows,* and the adventures of characters such as Sherlock Holmes, King Arthur, and Tarzan filled his mind with tales of excitement and bravery.

WHEN BRIAN WAS TEN YEARS OLD, HE WROTE A STORY ABOUT A BIRD THAT CLEANS A CROCODILE'S TEETH, AND HIS TEACHER ACCUSED HIM OF COPYING THE STORY FROM SOMEWHERE ELSE.

Attending St. John's, an inner-city school whose playground was on its roof, Brian Jacques began writing stories at the age of ten. His favorite teacher, Austin Thomas, introduced Brian to poetry and Greek literature when Brian was fourteen. At St. John's, he also met a teacher named Alan Durband, who many years later would have a profound impact on his life.

When Brian finished school at age fifteen, his craving for adventure led him to board a ship and set sail as a merchant seaman, a common occupation for young men in Liverpool. Brian traveled to faraway places such as New York, San Francisco, and Yokohama, Japan. But he soon tired of the lonely life of a sailor.

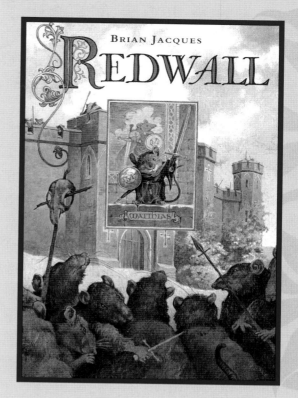

A Selected Bibliography of Jacques's Work

High Rhulain (2005)
Ribbajack and other Curious Yarns (2004)
Tribes of Redwall Mice (2003)
Triss: A Tale from Redwall (2002)
Castaways of the Flying Dutchman (2001)
A Redwall Winter's Tale (2001)
Taggerung: A Tale from Redwall (2001)
Lord Brocktree: A Tale of Redwall (2000)
The Legend of Luke (1999)
Marlfox (1999)
The Long Patrol: A Tale from Redwall (1997)
Pearls of Lutra (1997)
Outcast of Redwall (1996)
The Great Redwall Feast (1995)
The Bellmaker (1995)
Martin the Warrior (1993)
Salamandastron (1992)
Mariel of Redwall (1991)
Seven Strange & Ghostly Tales (1991)
Mattimeo (1990)
Mossflower (1988)
Redwall (1986)

> *"My ideas come crowding into my mind and then they clamour to be let out. I take my little West Highland terrier for a good long walk . . . and we talk it over, and then I sit down in my garden to write until the tale is done."*

Returning home to Liverpool, Jacques worked a variety of jobs and began writing music, poetry, and plays. While working as a truck driver, Jacques regularly delivered milk to the Royal Wavertree School for the Blind. He soon began volunteering his time to read to the students there. As he read, ideas for his own story began to form in his mind. He soon began writing the book that would become *Redwall.*

Jacques wrote *Redwall* for the children at the school, keeping his audience in mind. Writing for blind students, his style emerged, so that the students could imagine the action easily in their minds. The story was a huge hit with the children at the school.

Jacques had stayed in touch with his former teacher Alan Durband, who read *Redwall* and showed it to a publisher without telling him. The publisher loved the tale and signed Jacques to a five-book contract for the adventure series featuring the battle between the peaceful mice and the evil rats. Brian dedicated his 1995 book *The Bellmaker* to Durband.

Today, the series has grown to sixteen titles, with more in the works. The Redwall books have been translated into several languages, including

---

BEFORE BECOMING A FULL-TIME AUTHOR, BRIAN JACQUES WORKED AS A MERCHANT SEAMAN, A RAILWAY FIREMAN, A LONGSHOREMAN, A LONG-DISTANCE TRUCK DRIVER, A BUS DRIVER, A BOXER, A POLICEMAN, A POSTMASTER, AND A STAND-UP COMIC.

Dutch and Japanese. An animated television series on public television has brought the tales to an even wider audience.

By combining his childhood love of adventure stories with some real-life adventures of his own, Brian Jacques created a series to fire the imaginations of a new generation of young readers.

> *"Be good mice, don't be dirty rats. Remember, television can't take you places the way books can. So read, read, read. When you write, paint pictures with words."*

✦

WHERE TO FIND OUT MORE ABOUT BRIAN JACQUES

BOOK

Holtze, Sally Holmes, ed. *Seventh Book of Junior Authors & Illustrators.*
New York: H. W. Wilson Company, 1996.

WEB SITES

REDWALL ABBEY: THE OFFICIAL REDWALL WEB SITE
http://www.redwall.org/
For a biographical sketch of Brian Jacques, book information, descriptions of the Redwall characters, and transcripts of interviews with the author

SCHOLASTIC AUTHORS ONLINE
http://www2.scholastic.com/teachers/authorsandbooks/authorstudies/
authorhome.jhtml?authorID=46&collateralID=5192&displayName=Biography
To read a biographical sketch of Brian Jacques, a booklist, and an interview transcript

———

BRIAN JACQUES HOSTS A RADIO PROGRAM ON BBC RADIO MERSEYSIDE ON SUNDAY AFTERNOONS IN LIVERPOOL. ON HIS SHOW, JACQUES PERFORMS COMEDY AND PLAYS HIS FAVORITE MUSIC—MOSTLY OPERA. HE IS AN EXPERT ABOUT THE SUBJECT.

Angela Johnson

Born: June 18, 1961

Tell Me a Story, Mama is the title of Angela Johnson's first picture book. It is also the reason she became a writer—to tell stories. Although Johnson's books celebrate African American families, their themes of family love and understanding appeal to everyone.

Family has always been important to Angela Johnson. She comes from a close-knit family and a long line of storytellers. She was born on June 18, 1961, in Tuskegee, Alabama, to Arthur Johnson, an autoworker, and Truzetta (Hall) Johnson, an accountant. As soon as Angela could talk, she began telling stories. Her parents say that, when she was an infant, she would lie

JOHNSON HAS KEPT A DIARY OF HER EXPERIENCES
AND DREAMS SINCE SHE WAS EIGHT YEARS OLD.

awake in her crib telling stories to herself. As she got older, she never tired of listening to the stories her father and grandfather told. In time, storytelling became second nature to her.

Angela grew up in the small town of Shorter, Alabama, and attended Maple Grove School. When her family moved to Windham, Ohio, Angela attended Windham High School. There, she became interested in literature and poetry and began writing down her thoughts and feelings in a diary.

After graduating from high school in 1979, Johnson enrolled at Kent State University in Kent, Ohio. Thinking that she might like to become a teacher or social worker, Johnson chose to study education. But

> *"There is such a rich storytelling tradition in the African American culture. It's art, dance, and music all rolled into one. I am lucky to be part of this proud tradition."*

before completing her degree, she left Kent State to become a writer. For the next eight years, she worked at a variety of jobs to support herself. She was a child development worker with VISTA (Volunteers in Service to America) and a nanny.

In 1989, Johnson published her first book, *Tell Me a Story, Mama*. It is based on her relationship with her father and the stories he shared with her when she was a child. The success of this book enabled Johnson

IN 1999, JOHNSON RECEIVED A CORETTA SCOTT KING AWARD FOR HER BOOK *HEAVEN*. THE SAME YEAR, HER BOOK *THE OTHER SIDE: SHORTER POEMS* WAS HONORED AS A RUNNER-UP.

A Selected Bibliography of Johnson's Work

Lily Brown's Paintings (2006)

Sweet Smell of Roses (2005)

Violet's Music (2004)

The First Part Last (2003)

Just Like Josh Gibson (2003)

Looking for Red (2002)

Running Back to Ludie (2001)

Down the Winding Road (2000)

Maniac Monkeys on Magnolia Street (1999)

Gone from Home: Short Takes (1998)

Heaven (1998)

The Other Side: Shorter Poems (1998)

Songs of Faith (1998)

Daddy Calls Me Man (1997)

The Aunt in Our House (1996)

Shoes Like Miss Alice's (1995)

Joshua by the Sea (1994)

Joshua's Night Whispers (1994)

Mama Bird, Baby Birds (1994)

Toning the Sweep (1993)

Julius (1993)

The Leaving Morning (1992)

One of Three (1991)

Do Like Kyla (1990)

When I Am Old with You (1990)

Tell Me a Story, Mama (1989)

Johnson's Major Literary Awards

2004 Coretta Scott King Author Award

2004 Michael L. Printz Award
The First Part Last

1999 Coretta Scott King Author Award
Heaven

1999 Coretta Scott King Author Honor Book
The Other Side: Shorter Poems

1994 Coretta Scott King Author Award
Toning the Sweep

1991 Coretta Scott King Author Honor Book
When I Am Old with You

to quit her jobs and write full time. During the early 1990s, she published many books for young children about family life. Her book *Do Like Kyla* is about the love that two sisters share. *When I Am Old with You* is a story about a boy who dreams about growing old with his grandfather. And in the book *One of Three,* a girl shares the joys and frustrations of being the youngest of three sisters in a family.

> *"Family storytelling has been the overriding influence in my writing. While my book characters aren't actual living beings, they are part of wholes—my family, living and dead."*

After writing many successful picture books, Angela Johnson published her first novel for young adults in 1993. The novel, called *Toning the Sweep,* celebrates family and friendship. Following the publication of this book, Johnson became even better known as a writer of novels, short stories, and poetry for preteens and teenagers.

Angela Johnson still lives in Ohio, close to her family. She continues to write books for children. Her board books and picture books delight preschoolers and early readers. Her novels, short stories, and poetry books help young adults get through difficult times. Johnson is a gifted storyteller. Her tales capture the hearts of everyone.

❧

WHERE TO FIND OUT MORE ABOUT ANGELA JOHNSON

BOOK

Holtze, Sally Holmes, ed. *Seventh Book of Junior Authors & Illustrators.* New York: H. W. Wilson Company, 1996.

WEB SITES

AFRICAN AMERICAN LITERATURE BOOK CLUB
http://aalbc.com/authors/angela.htm
To read a biographical account of Angela Johnson and synopses of some of her books

HOUGHTON MIFFLIN: MEET THE AUTHOR
http://www.eduplace.com/kids/hmr/mtai/johnson.html
To read a biographical sketch of and booklist for Angela Johnson

―――

ONE OF ANGELA'S FAVORITE ACTIVITIES IN GRADE SCHOOL
WAS TO GO TO THE LOCAL DRUGSTORE TWICE A WEEK TO
BUY SNICKERS BARS AND ARCHIE COMIC BOOKS.

Ann Jonas

Born: January 28, 1932

For more than twenty years, Ann Jonas has been making creatively illustrated picture books for children. Her best-known books include *The Quilt; Round Trip; Bird Talk;* and *Aardvarks, Disembark!*

Ann Jonas was born on January 28, 1932, in Flushing, New York. She was taught to think creatively at an early age, since her parents preferred making their own clothes and furniture to buying them in a store. When not helping her parents, Ann and her brother spent many hours playing outdoors. They walked through the fields and parks. They loved to discover new things and use their imaginations. Today, imagination plays a big part in Jonas's books. In one story, she writes about a little girl who thinks

JONAS HAS TWO DAUGHTERS, NINA AND AMY.

gorillas are disguised as bushes and that chimneys look like giraffes.

In Ann's family, drawing was something you did while you were planning a project, not something you did just for its own sake. But Ann loved to draw and decided that she wanted to be an artist when she grew up.

After she finished high school, Jonas did not think about going to college. She got a job working in the advertising department of a department store. But she decided that she needed to know much more about art, so she went to art school. She met her husband while studying there. After she finished school, she got a job in a graphic design studio.

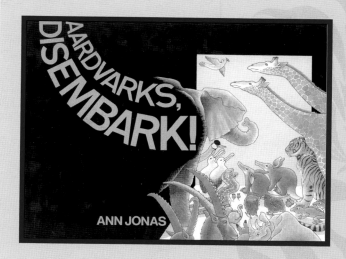

A Selected Bibliography of Jonas's Work

Stars Beneath Your Bed: The Surprising Story of Dust (2005)
Bird Talk (1999)
Watch William Walk (1997)
Splash! (1995)
The 13th Clue (1992)
Aardvarks, Disembark! (1990)
Color Dance (1989)
Reflections (1987)
Now We Can Go (1986)
Where Can It Be? (1986)
The Trek (1985)
Holes and Peeks (1984)
The Quilt (1984)
Round Trip (1983)
Two Bear Cubs (1982)
When You Were a Baby (1982)

Jonas's Major Literary Awards

1991 Boston Globe–Horn Book Picture Book Honor Book
   Aardvarks, Disembark!

1986 Boston Globe–Horn Book Picture Book Honor Book
   The Trek

In the early 1960s, her husband was drafted into the army. They moved to Germany for several years. Jonas worked for an advertising agency while living in Germany. When they returned to the United States, Jonas and her husband opened their own graphic design studio.

Jonas's husband began writing and illustrating books for children. He encouraged Jonas to try to write a children's book. He introduced her to a publisher, who also urged her to write a book. Her first book, *When You Were a Baby,* was published in 1982. The book was success-ful, and Jonas decided to become a full-time children's book writer and illustrator.

"I find that I approach each book quite differently. Each idea seems to need a specific technique and style to most clearly illustrate the point I'm trying to make."

Jonas uses many differ-ent styles of illustration for her books and tries to come up with creative ways of making the books interesting for children. Her book *Round Trip* describes a trip from the country to the city. At the end of the book, it can be turned upside down and read backward. When the book is turned over, the story describes the trip back to the country. It took Jonas a long time to get this book just right. *Color Dance* also uses an imaginative technique to get readers' attention.

———

JONAS'S BOOK *THE QUILT* WAS WRITTEN FOR HER DAUGHTER, NINA. IT IS BASED ON A QUILT THAT JONAS MADE FOR HER.

As three dancers wave multicolored scarves through the air, children get to learn about different color combinations.

Jonas continues to write and illustrate picture books for children. She lives in New York with her family.

⁂

WHERE TO FIND OUT MORE ABOUT ANN JONAS

BOOKS

Holtze, Sally Holmes, ed. *Seventh Book of Junior Authors & Illustrators.* H. W. Wilson Company: New York, 1996.

McElmeel, Sharron L. *100 Most Popular Picture Book Authors and Illustrators: Biographical Sketches and Bibliographies.* Englewood, Colo.: Libraries Unlimited, 2000.

Silvey, Anita, ed. *The Essential Guide to Children's Books and Their Creators.* Boston: Houghton Mifflin Company, 2002.

WEB SITES

HARPER CHILDREN'S
http://www.harperchildrens.com/teacher/catalog/author_xml.asp?authorID=17146
To read a biographical sketch of Ann Jonas

NATIONAL CENTER FOR CHILDREN'S ILLUSTRATED LITERATURE
http://www.nccil.org/jonas.html
To read a biography of Ann Jonas

WHEN WRITING THE BOOK *AARDVARKS, DISEMBARK!* JONAS LEARNED ABOUT THE NUMBER OF ANIMALS THAT ARE NOW EXTINCT OR ENDANGERED. SHE USED THE BOOK AS A WAY TO TEACH CHILDREN ABOUT PROTECTING THEM.

William Joyce

Born: December 11, 1957

n William Joyce's books, anything can happen. Dinosaurs dance the hokey-pokey. Gorillas wear ties and walk down the street. Uncles ride in flying saucers. How does Joyce explain such bizarre happenings? He says he is simply fighting for "the cause of global silliness."

William Joyce was born on December 11, 1957, in Shreveport, Louisiana. From an early age, he showed a talent for drawing. Art was his favorite subject in school. He spent much of his time as a boy drawing sketches. He started drawing dogs and cats, but

---

JOYCE WAS ONE OF SEVERAL ILLUSTRATORS WHO WORKED ON THE MOVIE *TOY STORY*.

before long he was drawing dinosaurs and spaceships. When William wasn't drawing, he was reading and watching movies and television. This helped shape his artistic imagination. He decided to study film-making at Southern Methodist University. But he hoped one day to write and illustrate his own books.

Even before Joyce graduated from college, he began seeking work as an illustrator. He sent samples of his work to publishers. He succeeded in landing a number of assignments to illustrate books by other authors. Joyce was not satisfied, though. He wanted to illustrate his own stories.

He finally got his chance when *George Shrinks* was published in 1985. The book tells the story of a boy who wakes up to find that he has shrunk overnight. Three-inch-tall George finds himself in the middle of new adventures because

> *"My characters are willing to fight for the right to act odd and suave."*

of his size. He dives into a goldfish bowl to feed his pet fish. He saddles his baby brother and rides on his back. *George Shrinks* won a Best Book Award from the *School Library Journal*.

Joyce's next book was *Dinosaur Bob and His Adventures with the Family Lazardo*. In the book, the Lazardos adopt Bob the Dinosaur after they meet him on their annual safari. Bob moves into the family's home in the suburbs, and soon displays a talent for baseball. The book was

---

JOYCE HAS CREATED ILLUSTRATIONS FOR
THE *NEW YORKER* AND OTHER MAGAZINES.

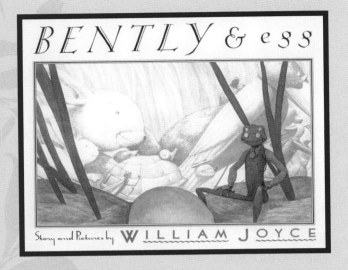

BENTLY & egg

Story and Pictures by WILLIAM JOYCE

A Selected Bibliography of Joyce's Work

Meet the Robinsons (2006)
Art of Robots (2005)
Big Time Olie (2002)
Peekaboo, You (2002)
Sleepy Time Olie (2001)
Snowie Rolie (2000)
Baseball Bob (1999)
Rolie Polie Olie (1999)
Life with Bob (1998)
Buddy (1997)
The World of William Joyce Scrapbook (1997)
The Leaf Men and the Brave Good Bugs (1996)
Santa Calls (1993)
Bently & Egg (1992)
A Day with Wilbur Robinson (1990)
Dinosaur Bob and His Adventures with the Family Lazardo (1988)
George Shrinks (1985)

very successful, and Bob became one of Joyce's most popular creations. Joyce has written two more books about Bob: *Life with Bob* and *Baseball Bob.*

Joyce created an unusual cast of characters for his next book. In *A Day with Wilbur Robinson,* frogs ride on dogs, goldfish are giants, and lovable uncles keep flying saucers parked behind the house. *A Day with Wilbur Robinson* won a Parents' Choice Award for 1991. Joyce followed that with *Bently & Egg.* Bently is a frog who tries to help his friend Kack Kack the Duck by egg-sitting. In 1993, Joyce published *Santa Calls,* about a brother and sister called to the North Pole by Santa Claus.

Joyce depends on his family for inspiration for his stories. Sometimes Joyce's wife, Elizabeth, will pose for him when he is trying to draw a new character. One of Joyce's stories had its beginnings in a bedtime story he told his daughter, Mary Katherine. That story became *The Leaf Men and the Brave Good Bugs.* It tells the story of the battle between the Leaf Men and the evil Spider Queen to save an elderly woman's rose garden.

"My dad says I was born with a pencil in my hand. I always loved drawing."

WHERE TO FIND OUT MORE ABOUT WILLIAM JOYCE

BOOKS

Holtze, Sally Holmes, ed. *Sixth Book of Junior Authors & Illustrators.* New York: H. W. Wilson Company, 1989.

Silvey, Anita, ed. *The Essential Guide to Children's Books and Their Creators.* Boston: Houghton Mifflin Company, 2002.

WEB SITES

THE BOOK PAGE
http://www.bookpage.com/9610bp/childrens/theleafmen.html
For an interview with William Joyce and information on
The Leaf Men and the Brave Good Bugs

HARPERCHILDRENS.COM
http://www.harperchildrens.com/hch/author/author/joyce/
To read a biographical sketch of William Joyce and synopses of his books

JOYCE'S BOOK *ROLIE POLIE OLIE* IS BASED ON A TELEVISION PROGRAM THAT JOYCE PRODUCED.

Norton Juster

Born: June 2, 1929

Norton Juster calls himself an accidental writer. For most of his adult life, he enjoyed a career as an architect. He only began writing as an escape from his regular work. Fortunately, this escape produced *The Phantom Tollbooth*. Now a classic children's fantasy, it has been popular with both children and adults for more than forty years.

Norton Juster was born in 1929 in Brooklyn, New York. His family owned a set of encyclopedias, and Norton liked to sit and read them just for fun. His father often made wordplay jokes. Norton didn't always understand them, but puns and other wordplay humor later became a big part of *The Phantom Tollbooth*'s appeal.

Norton attended public schools in New York City. He earned his degree in architecture from the University of Pennsylvania in 1952. Then he

JUSTER LOVES COOKING AND IS PROUD OF THE PICKLES, JAM, AND MARMALADE HE MAKES.

won a Fulbright scholarship, which allowed him to attend school outside the United States. So he spent a year studying city planning at the University of Liverpool in England.

Juster served in the U.S. Navy from 1954 to 1957. Then he began working as an architect. He also began writing stories in his spare time. His masterpiece, *The Phantom Tollbooth*, came out in 1961. It follows the oddball adventures of a boy named Milo, who rides his electric car through a tollbooth into a strange world. Milo's companion on this journey is Tock, the ticking watchdog.

While he was writing the book, Juster lived in a rundown apartment in Brooklyn Heights, New York. He paced back and

A Selected Bibliography of Juster's Work

The Hello, Goodbye Window (2005)
As Silly As Knees, As Busy As Bees (1998)
As: A Surfeit of Similes (1989)
Otter Nonsense (1982)
Alberic the Wise (1965)
The Dot and the Line: A Romance in Lower Mathematics (1963)
The Phantom Tollbooth (1961)

Juster's Major Literary Awards

2005 Boston Globe-Horn Book Picture Book Honor Book
   The Hello, Goodbye Window

> *"When I wrote* The Phantom Tollbooth, *I didn't know I was writing a book. I thought I was trying to avoid working on something else."*

forth as he wrote, and his footsteps bothered his downstairs neighbor, cartoonist Jules Feiffer. Feiffer came up to see what Juster was working on. He liked the book and ended up drawing the illustrations for it.

The Dot and the Line was Juster's next book. It's about a straight line who is in love with a dot. The dot, however, is in love with a squiggle.

Juster married graphic designer Jeanne Ray in 1964, and they had a daughter named Emily. Juster continued working as an architect and also taught design at the Pratt Institute in Brooklyn, New York. In 1970, the family bought a farm in Buckland, Massachusetts. After ten years on the farm, they moved to the town of Amherst, Massachusetts, so Emily could be closer to friends and activities.

Juster got the idea for his book *The Hello, Goodbye Window* from spending time with his granddaughter, Tori. In the story, a little girl spends the night with her grandparents, who have a magical kitchen window.

> *"My idea of a perfect world would be to have an endless amount of work surfaces or a series of rooms so that I could just move on to the next one when one gets filled with stuff."*

JUSTER TAUGHT ARCHITECTURE AND ENVIRONMENTAL DESIGN AT HAMPSHIRE COLLEGE IN AMHERST, MASSACHUSETTS, FROM 1970 TO 1992.

Juster is retired as an architect now, but he still works on his books in Amherst.

༂

WHERE TO FIND OUT MORE ABOUT NORTON JUSTER

BOOKS

Berger, Laura Standley, ed. *Twentieth-Century Young Adult Writers.* 1st ed. Detroit: St. James Press, 1994.

Pringle, David, ed. *St. James Guide to Fantasy Writers.* Detroit: St. James Press, 1996.

Silvey, Anita, ed. *The Essential Guide to Children's Books and Their Creators.* Boston: Houghton Mifflin Company, 2002.

WEB SITES

ABSOLUTE WRITE
http://www.absolutewrite.com/novels/norton_juster.htm
For an interview with Norton Juster

KIRKUS REVIEWS
http://www.thebookstandard.com/bookstandard/news/author/article_ display.jsp?vnu_content_id=1001570449
For a synopsis of the author's latest award-winning book and an interview

JUSTER WAS NOT THE ONLY ARCHITECT IN HIS FAMILY. HIS FATHER AND BROTHER WERE ARCHITECTS, TOO.

Cynthia Kadohata

Born: July 2, 1956

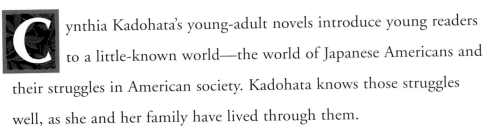

Cynthia Kadohata's young-adult novels introduce young readers to a little-known world—the world of Japanese Americans and their struggles in American society. Kadohata knows those struggles well, as she and her family have lived through them.

Cynthia's father's parents were immigrants from Japan, and her mother's family, also Japanese, lived in Hawaii. Her parents made their home in Chicago, Illinois, where Cynthia was born in 1956. When she was a child, her family moved around as her father looked for jobs. In Georgia and Arkansas, he worked as a chicken sexer. (That's a person who determines the sex of chicks in a chicken hatchery so they can be separated and fed differently.)

Cynthia was painfully shy when she was growing up. As she recalls,

DURING WORLD WAR II (1939–1945), JAPANESE AMERICANS CONSIDERED A THREAT TO NATIONAL SECURITY WERE IMPRISONED IN CAMPS. KADOHATA'S FATHER WAS HELD IN A CAMP IN POSTON, ARIZONA. THE POSTON CAMP INSPIRED KADOHATA'S NOVEL *WEEDFLOWER*.

"It got to the point that going to the grocery store and talking to the cashier really made me nervous." When she was reading, she was comfortably alone. Cynthia loved animals and reading about them. Among her favorite books were animal stories such as *The Call*

> "I had always thought that nonfiction represented the 'truth.' . . . [Then] I realized you could say things with fiction that you couldn't say any other way."

of the Wild and *White Fang* by Jack London and *King of the Wind* by Marguerite Henry.

When Cynthia was fifteen, the family settled in Los Angeles, California. After high school, she held various part-time jobs as a waitress and a department-store clerk. Then she enrolled in Los Angeles City College. She eventually transferred to the University of Southern California in Los Angeles, receiving a degree in journalism in 1977.

At twenty-four, Kadohata sensed that she had no direction in life. Searching for inspiration, she took a Greyhound bus trip up and down the West Coast and into the southern and southwestern United States. Then she decided to start writing in earnest.

Kadohata moved to Boston, Massachusetts, and took temporary office jobs while working on her writing. Her plan of action was to write

---

KADOHATA'S FIRST REJECTION CAME FROM THE *ATLANTIC MONTHLY* MAGAZINE
FOR HER SHORT STORY "THE ONE-LEGGED DUCKS" ABOUT
A PLANET POPULATED BY ONE-LEGGED DUCKS.

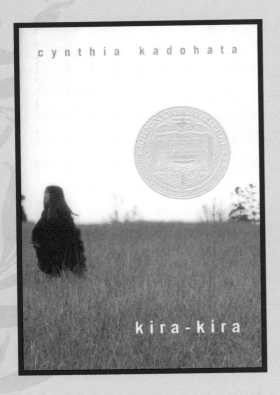

c y n t h i a   k a d o h a t a

k i r a - k i r a

A Selected Bibliography of Kadohata's Work

Weedflower (2006)
The Glass Mountains (2004)
Kira-Kira (2004)

Kadohata's Major Literary Awards

2005 Newbery Medal
 Kira-Kira

one short story a month and submit each to magazines. This resulted in about forty-eight rejections. Finally, after rejecting twenty-five of her stories, the *New Yorker* magazine accepted one in 1986.

Kadohata decided to polish her skills by enrolling in fiction-writing programs at the University of Pittsburgh and Columbia University in New York City. As more of her short stories were published, an agent encouraged her to try writing

"Just thinking about the American landscape and focusing on it puts me in touch with what I think of as the real, essential me."

books. Kadohata did just that, producing the adult novels *The Floating World* (1989) and *In the Heart of the Valley of Love* (1992). She wove many of her personal experiences into both novels.

In 2004, Kadohata adopted a baby boy, Sammy, from the central Asian republic of Kazakhstan. Her young-adult novel *Kira-Kira* was published that same year. It's the story of a Japanese American girl growing up in the American South. In writing the book, Kadohata was inspired by her own childhood, and she includes many childhood memories in the story. *Weedflower*, published in 2006, explores the friendship between a Japanese American girl and a Native American boy.

Today, Cynthia Kadohata lives near Los Angeles. She likes writing outdoors with her dog by her side.

❧

WHERE TO FIND OUT MORE ABOUT CYNTHIA KADOHATA

WEB SITES

CYNTHIA KADOHATA
http://www.kira-kira.us/index.html
For a biography, a glimpse into the author's personal life, and an interview

TIME FOR KIDS
http://www.timeforkids.com/TFK/kidscoops/story/0,14989,1028042,00.html
For an interview with Cynthia Kadohata

KADOHATA'S DOG IS A DOBERMAN PINSCHER NAMED SHIKA KOJIKA. THAT'S JAPANESE FOR "DEER, LITTLE DEER."

Ezra Jack Keats

Born: March 11, 1916
Died: May 6, 1983

zra Jack Keats was one of the first American children's authors

to use an African American child as the key character in a book.

Keats's award-winning book *The Snowy Day* features a young black boy

named Peter. Keats also used Peter in

other books. Along with illustrating

numerous books for other authors,

Keats wrote many of his own books

including *Whistle for Willie, A Letter to*

Amy, and *Goggles.*

Ezra Jack Keats was born on

March 11, 1916, in Brooklyn, New York. At an early age, Keats was

interested in being an artist. His mother encouraged him to work on his

drawings. She appreciated her son's talent as an artist. Keats's father had

a different idea.

KEATS'S PARENTS WERE BORN IN POLAND AND DID NOT MEET UNTIL
THEY CAME TO THE UNITED STATES. A MATCHMAKER ARRANGED THEIR WEDDING.

He told his son that he could not be successful as an artist. He wanted his son to learn how to do something so he could earn a living. Keats finally convinced his father that he could make money being an artist when he was paid twenty-five cents to paint a sign for a candy store. His father was pleased and was sure he could earn a living as a sign painter.

When Keats graduated from high school, he was awarded a medal for his art. He was unable to share the medal with his father. Keats's father had died the day before. Keats also received scholarships to attend art schools. He was unable to accept the scholarships because he needed to

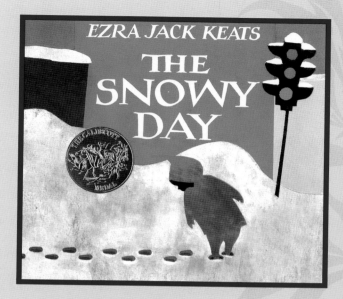

A Selected Bibliography of Keats's Work

One Red Sun: A Counting Book (1999)
Song of the River (Illustrations only, 1993)
Clementina's Cactus (1982)
Louie's Search (1980)
Pet Show! (1972)
Apt. 3 (1971)
Over in the Meadow (1971)
Hi, Cat! (1970)
Goggles (1969)
A Letter to Amy (1968)
John Henry, an American Legend (1965)
Whistle for Willie (1964)
The Snowy Day (1962)
My Dog Is Lost! (With Pat Scherr, 1960)
Jubilant for Sure (Illustrations only, 1954)

Keats's Major Literary Awards

1970 Boston Globe-Horn Book Picture Book Honor Book
  Hi, Cat!
1970 Caldecott Honor Book
  Goggles
1963 Caldecott Medal
  The Snowy Day

> "*Then began an experience that turned my life around—working on a book with a black kid as hero. None of the manuscripts I'd been illustrating featured any black kids. . . . My book would have him there simply because he should have been there all along.*"

get a job to support his family.

In 1937, Keats got a job as a mural painter and took art classes at night. Three years later, he became an illustrator for a company that published comic books. In 1943, he joined the army and used his skills as an artist to design camouflage patterns.

After Keats left the army, he went to Paris, France, to study art and to work on his paintings. Many of his paintings would later be displayed in New York art galleries. When he returned to New York, he decided to pursue a career as an illustrator. He painted covers and illustrations for several magazines. He also sold some of his paintings.

In 1954, Keats illustrated *Jubilant for Sure,* a children's book written by Elisabeth Hubbard Lansing. He continued to illustrate many other children's books for other authors. Keats's first book—

> "*I didn't even ask to get into children's books.*"

KEATS'S FAMILY HAD MANY TALENTED ARTISTS. HIS BROTHER BECAME A PORTRAIT PHOTOGRAPHER, AND HIS SISTER BECAME A SCULPTOR.

My Dog Is Lost!—was cowritten with Pat Scherr and was published in 1960.

Keats used a special art technique to illustrate his books. He used collages and gouache. Gouache is an opaque watercolor paint mixed with a gum that produces a glaze on the pictures. This technique makes Keats's illustrations very different from those in other books.

Keats wrote and illustrated twenty-three children's books. He never married or had children. He died in New York on May 6, 1983.

WHERE TO FIND OUT MORE ABOUT EZRA JACK KEATS

BOOKS

Kovacs, Deborah, and James Preller. *Meet the Authors and Illustrators: 60 Creators of Favorite Children's Books Talk about Their Work.* Vol. 1. New York: Scholastic, 1991.

McElmeel, Sharron L. *100 Most Popular Picture Book Authors and Illustrators: Biographical Sketches and Bibliographies.* Englewood, Colo.: Libraries Unlimited, 2000.

Silvey, Anita, ed. *The Essential Guide to Children's Books and Their Creators.* Boston: Houghton Mifflin Company, 2002.

WEB SITES

EZRA JACK KEATS FOUNDATION
http://www.ezra-jack-keats.org/
For information about Ezra Jack Keats and his foundation

UNIVERSITY OF SOUTHERN MISSISSIPPI DE GRUMMOND COLLECTION
http://www.lib.usm.edu/~degrum/keats/main.html
To read a biographical sketch of Ezra Jack Keats, a booklist, and a description of the making of an Ezra Jack Keats picture book

KEATS WAS JEWISH, AND HIS NAME AT BIRTH WAS JACOB KATZ. AFTER WORLD WAR II (1939–1945), HE LEGALLY CHANGED HIS NAME TO EZRA JACK KEATS BECAUSE HE WAS CONCERNED HOW HE WOULD BE TREATED IF PEOPLE KNEW HE WAS JEWISH.

Steven Kellogg

Born: October 26, 1941

teven Kellogg's job lets him do something he loves—make up stories and draw pictures. Steven has loved to draw since he was a boy. He drew the things he saw around him. He drew the things he saw in books. He drew for his grandma, who was his best friend. He made up stories for his younger sisters. While telling them the stories, he drew pictures at the same time. His sisters called this "telling stories on paper."

Steven was born on October 26, 1941, in Norwalk, Connecticut. As a child, he enjoyed picture books. Animal stories were his favorite. After graduating from high school, Kellogg went to the Rhode

KELLOGG BELIEVES IT IS VERY IMPORTANT FOR ADULTS AND CHILDREN TO SHARE PICTURE BOOKS TOGETHER.

Island School of Design in Providence. He decided to concentrate on studying the art of illustration. Illustration is drawing pictures, usually to go along with a story. During his last year at the Rhode Island School of Design, he was able to live and study in Florence, Italy. That year was very important to him. His experiences in Italy have left him with many memories. He uses these memories as he writes and illustrates his books.

> *"I want the time that the reader shares with me and my work to be an enjoyable experience—one that will encourage a lifetime association with pictures, words, and books."*

Kellogg started his publishing career by illustrating books that were written by other people. In 1967, his first book of illustrations was published. It was called *Gwot! Horribly Funny Hairticklers.* Although he was good at illustrating stories written by other people, he was also interested in writing the stories himself. His first story, *The Wicked Kings of Bloon,* was published in 1970. Since then, Kellogg has had more than 100 books published.

The ideas for Kellogg's books come from many places. One famous character in Kellogg's books is Pinkerton the dog. Pinkerton is not a pretend character. He is Kellogg's real-life dog. Kellogg wrote

ROSE, THE CAT IN *A ROSE FOR PINKERTON*, WAS REALLY KELLOGG'S OLD GROUCHY CAT!

A Selected Bibliography of Kellogg's Work

Invisible Moose (Illustrations only, 2006)

Clorinda the Fearless (Illustrations only, 2005)

Clorinda (2002)

A Penguin Pup for Pinkerton (2001)

The Missing Mitten Mystery (2000)

Three Sillies (1999)

The Three Little Pigs (1997)

Frogs Jump: A Counting Book (1996)

Parents in the Pigpen, Pigs in the Tub (1993)

Johnny Appleseed: A Tall Tale (1988)

Pecos Bill: A Tall Tale (1986)

How Much Is a Million? (1985)

Paul Bunyan: A Tall Tale (1984)

A Rose for Pinkerton (1981)

The Day Jimmy's Boa Ate the Wash (1980)

Pinkerton, Behave! (1979)

The Mysterious Tadpole (1977)

The Boy Who Was Followed Home (1975)

The Wicked Kings of Bloon (1970)

Gwot! Horribly Funny Hairticklers (Illustrations only, 1967)

Kellogg's Major Literary Award

1985 Boston Globe-Horn Book Picture Book Honor Book
  How Much Is a Million?

these books with the ideas he got from living with Pinkerton.

People enjoy Kellogg's stories and illustrations for several reasons. Kellogg uses humor in his writing and in the illustrations. The illustrations are also colorful and usually fill the entire page. The characters are drawn in a way that gives them movement and life.

Kellogg puts a lot of work into making sure that his pictures add to the words of

> *"The pictures are compelling and important and they offer kids an opportunity to journey into themselves and provide an avenue for escape."*

the story. The pictures actually become part of the story. He sees the pictures and words like different musical instruments playing together to produce something wonderful.

☙

WHERE TO FIND OUT MORE ABOUT STEVEN KELLOGG

BOOKS

Collier, Laurie, and Joyce Nakamura, eds. *Major Authors and Illustrators for Children and Young Adults.* Detroit: Gale Research, 1993.

Kovacs, Deborah, and James Preller. *Meet the Authors and Illustrators: 60 Creators of Favorite Children's Books Talk about Their Work.* Vol. 1. New York: Scholastic, 1991.

McElmeel, Sharron L. *100 Most Popular Picture Book Authors and Illustrators: Biographical Sketches and Bibliographies.* Englewood, Colo.: Libraries Unlimited, 2000.

Rockman, Connie C., ed. *The Ninth Book of Junior Authors and Illustrators.* New York: H. W. Wilson Company, 2004.

WEB SITES

EDUCATIONAL PAPERBACK ASSOCIATION
http://edupaperback.org/showauth.cfm?authid=143
To read an autobiographical sketch and booklist for Steven Kellogg

STEVEN KELLOGG HOME PAGE
http://www.stevenkellogg.com
To read more about Steven Kellogg, to see a gallery of his book covers, and to find out how to contact him

———

KELLOGG HAS BEEN AN ETCHING INSTRUCTOR AT AMERICAN UNIVERSITY AND HAS TAUGHT PRINTMAKING AND PAINTING.

X. J. Kennedy
Dorothy M. Kennedy

Born: August 21, 1929 (X. J.)
Born: March 8, 1931 (Dorothy)

For many children, their first exposure to poetry is a playful, whimsical, joyful experience. That's sure to be the case if the poetry is served up by X. J. and Dorothy Kennedy. This husband-and-wife team has published many delightful collections of poetry for children.

X. J. Kennedy was born Joseph Charles Kennedy in Dover, New Jersey, in 1929. As a toddler, little Joe sat in his high chair scribbling for hours with a pencil and paper. His father loved poetry and often recited verses for the family. Joe himself liked to sit and read poetry from a large anthology, or collection, the family owned. By the time he was in high school, Joe's favorite literature was science fiction.

Joe attended Seton Hall College in nearby South Orange, New Jersey. One summer, he sold two stories to science fiction magazines. After graduating in 1950, he earned a master's degree at Columbia University in New York City. Then he joined the U.S. Navy, serving as a journalist.

X. J. KENNEDY TAUGHT ENGLISH AT TUFTS UNIVERSITY FROM 1963 THROUGH 1979.

Joe had never lost his love for poetry, and while he was in the Navy, his first published poem appeared in the *New Yorker* magazine. By that point, he was tired of jokes that he was related to Joseph P. Kennedy, the father of future U.S. president John Kennedy. So he began using the pen name X. J. Kennedy.

After studying for a year in Paris, France, Kennedy enrolled in graduate school at the University of Michigan in Ann Arbor. That's where he met Dorothy Mintzlaff.

Dorothy, born in 1931, was raised in Milwaukee, Wisconsin. She attended Milwaukee-Downer College, graduating in 1953. For the

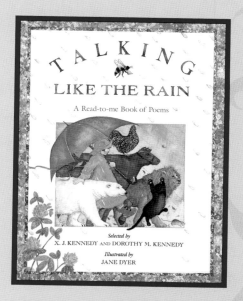

A Selected Bibliography of the Kennedys' Work

Joint works
Knee-Deep in Blazing Snow (editors, 2005)
Talking Like the Rain: A Read-to-Me Book of Poems (editors, 1992)
Knock at a Star: A Child's Introduction to Poetry (editors, 1982)

X. J. Kennedy's works
Exploding Gravy: Poems to Make You Laugh (2002)
The Eagle As Wide As the World (1997)
The Beasts of Bethlehem (1993)
One Winter Night in August and Other Nonsense Jingles (1975)

Dorothy Kennedy's works
Make Things Fly (editor, 1998)
I Thought I'd Take My Rat to School (editor, 1983)

> *"Writing verse for children calls for just as much work as writing verse for adults. The nice thing about children is that they do not give a hoot about literary fashion."*
> —X. J. Kennedy

next two years, she taught high school English and Spanish in Milledgeville, Illinois. She earned her master's degree from the University of Michigan in Ann Arbor in 1956. Later, while teaching there, she met X. J. The two were married in 1962.

In 1963, the Kennedys moved to Massachusetts, where X. J. taught English at Tufts University in Medford, writing poetry and college textbooks at the same time. In 1975, he published the first book of his own poems for children—*One Winter Night in August and Other Nonsense Jingles.*

Meanwhile, the Kennedys were raising one daughter and four sons. When their youngest child started school in the late 1970s, Dorothy turned her attention to writing. She and X. J. were both writing textbooks when they decided to assemble a collection of poetry for children. It was published as *Knock at a Star: A Child's Introduction to Poetry* in 1982. Their next poetry collection was *Talking Like the Rain: A Read-to-Me Book of Poems.*

The two worked on many other projects, both separately and together. X. J. wrote children's poetry and more textbooks. Together, he and Dorothy together wrote textbooks for fiction and creative writing

---

IN THE 1970S, THE KENNEDYS PUBLISHED A POETRY MAGAZINE CALLED *COUNTER/MEASURES: A MAGAZINE OF RIME, METER, AND SONG.*

courses. Dorothy's first solo book, *I Thought I'd Take My Rat to School*, came out in 1993. It's a collection of poems about kids' school life. Her next book, *Make Things Fly*, contains poems about the wind. The Kennedys now live in Lexington, Massachusetts.

> *"As a writer I bloomed late—maybe because I can't seem to bloom in more than one area at a time."*
> —Dorothy M. Kennedy

WHERE TO FIND OUT MORE ABOUT X. J. KENNEDY AND DOROTHY M. KENNEDY

BOOKS

Rockman, Connie C., ed. *The Ninth Book of Junior Authors and Illustrators.*
New York: H. W. Wilson Company, 2004.

Silvey, Anita, ed. *The Essential Guide to Children's Books and Their Creators.*
Boston: Houghton Mifflin Company, 2002.

WEB SITES

EDUCATION OASIS: CHILDREN'S BOOK REVIEWS
http://www.educationoasis.com/ch_book_reviews/reviews/talking_like_rain.htm
For a review of *Talking Like the Rain: A Read-to-Me Book of Poems*

NATIONAL COUNCIL OF TEACHERS OF ENGLISH
http://www.ncte.org/elem/awards/poetry/113272.htm
To read about X. J. Kennedy's 2000 Poetry Award

X. J. AND DOROTHY M. KENNEDY HOME PAGE
http://www.xjanddorothymkennedy.com/
For a biography about each writer, a list of books for children and adults, and current news

---

A COLONY OF RABBITS LIVES UNDER THE FRONT PORCH
OF THE KENNEDYS' ONE-HUNDRED-YEAR-OLD HOUSE.

M. E. Kerr

Born: May 27, 1927

As a writer, M. E. Kerr uses many different names. Her real name is Marijane Meaker. She uses the name M. E. Kerr when she writes novels for young adults. She has also written using the names M. J. Meaker, Mary James, Ann Aldrich, and Vin Packer. Kerr's most popular books include *The Son of Someone Famous, Little Little, What I Really Think of You,* and *Night Kites.*

M. E. Kerr was born on May 27, 1927, in Auburn, New York. Her father loved to read and write and had many books in the house. Kerr shared her father's love of writing. She loved to read and was encouraged by her teachers and librarians. Kerr knew at a young age that she wanted to be a writer.

She was not a very good student in school. She was always getting in trouble. Kerr's parents

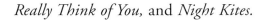

AFTER COLLEGE, KERR SENT STORIES TO MAGAZINES, BUT SHE RECEIVED MANY REJECTION LETTERS. ONE YEAR FOR A HALLOWEEN PARTY, SHE COVERED HERSELF WITH THE LETTERS SHE HAD RECEIVED AND WENT AS A REJECTION NOTICE.

became frustrated with her. They wanted her to be a better student. When she was a teenager, Kerr was sent to a boarding school in Virginia. During the summers, she wrote many stories. She sent them to magazines, but none of the stories was published. Attending a new school did not help Kerr's behavior. She continued to get into trouble. Even though she was suspended during her senior year, Kerr graduated from the school.

Kerr attended a junior college for a short time. She worked on the newspaper at the college. In 1946, she transferred to the University of Missouri. She started as a journalism student but soon switched

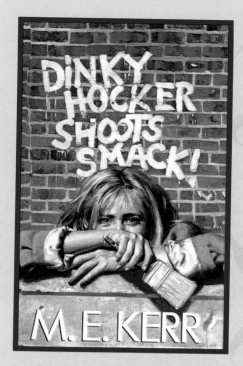

A Selected Bibliography of Kerr's Work

Your Eyes in Stars: A Novel (2006)

Snakes Don't Miss Their Mothers: A Novel (2003)

Books of Fell (2001)

Slap Your Sides (2001)

What Became of Her (2000)

Blood on the Forehead: What I Know about Writing (1998)

"Hello," I Lied (1997)

Deliver Us from Evie (1994)

Linger (1993)

Fell Back (1989)

Night Kites (1986)

What I Really Think of You (1982)

Little Little (1981)

Gentle Hands (1978)

The Son of Someone Famous (1974)

Dinky Hocker Shoots Smack (1972)

> *"When I write for young adults I know they're still wrestling with . . . problems like winning and losing, not feeling accepted or accepting, prejudice, love. . . . I know my audience hasn't yet made up their minds about everything. . . . Give me that kind of audience any day!"*

to studying English. She wanted to be a fiction writer. When she finished college, she moved to New York and got a job with a publishing company.

Kerr continued to write stories and send them to publishers. Finally, in 1951, she got her first story published in a magazine. This was the start of Kerr's writing career. She wrote several novels and nonfiction books for adults during the next several years.

One of her books included a main character who was a teenager. Kerr's friends encouraged her to write a novel for young adults. She decided to use the name M. E. Kerr for this novel. The book, *Dinky Hocker Shoots Smack,* was published in 1972. Since then, she has published many novels for young adults.

> *"When I think of myself and what I would have liked to have found in books those many years ago, I remember being depressed by all the neatly tied-up, happy-ending stories, the abundance of winners, the themes of winning, solving, finding—when around me it didn't seem that easy."*

KERR'S NOVELS APPEAL TO BOTH BOYS AND GIRLS. SHE USUALLY WRITES FROM THE MALE VIEWPOINT BECAUSE SHE HAS FOUND THAT BOYS WILL NOT READ A BOOK WITH A FEMALE MAIN CHARACTER.

Kerr's novels are about real issues that kids experience. She uses humor in her books. She also writes about serious issues. Her books have dealt with such issues as mental illness, sexuality, drug addiction, and racism. She gets many of the ideas for her books from her own memories of being young.

Kerr continues to write for young adults and others. She lives in East Hampton, New York.

❧

WHERE TO FIND OUT MORE ABOUT M. E. KERR

BOOKS

Kerr, M. E. *Blood on the Forehead: What I Know about Writing.*
New York: HarperCollins, 1998.

Kerr, M. E. *Me, Me, Me, Me, Me: Not a Novel.*
New York: Harper & Row, 1983.

Sutherland, Zena. *Children & Books.*
New York: Addison Wesley Longman, 1997.

WEB SITES

THE M. E. KERR AND MARY JAMES HOME PAGE
http://www.mekerr.com/
For a biography of M. E. Kerr, information about her books, and reviews

VANDERGRIFT YOUNG ADULT LITERATURE PAGE
http://scils.rutgers.edu/~kvander/kerr.html
To read a detailed biographical sketch of M. E. Kerr, a booklist,
and a summary of her awards

———

KERR WAS GOOD FRIENDS WITH LOUISE FITZHUGH, THE AUTHOR OF *HARRIET THE SPY*. FITZHUGH WAS ONE OF THE PEOPLE WHO ENCOURAGED KERR TO WRITE NOVELS FOR YOUNG ADULTS.

Eric Kimmel

Born: October 30, 1946

As a young boy, Eric Kimmel dreamed of seeing his name on the cover of a book. He remembers his kindergarten teacher telling the class that one of them could write a book. He was excited by that thought. He decided that he wanted to be a writer even before he knew how to write. Kimmel has been writing books for children and young people for more than twenty-five years. His best-known books include *Sirko and the Wolf: A Ukrainian Tale; Boots and His Brothers: A Norwegian Tale; Anansi and the Talking Melon;* and *Bearhead: A Russian Folktale.*

Eric Kimmel was born on October 30, 1946, in Brooklyn, New York. He loved to read books and write stories as a child. "Somehow, I

BEFORE WRITING A STORY, KIMMEL MAY THINK ABOUT IT FOR SEVERAL YEARS.

always knew that I was going to be a writer when I grew up, and that I would share the stories I loved so much with others," Kimmel says. He especially loved reading books by Dr. Seuss. His favorite was *Horton Hatches the Egg*.

He also loved listening to his grandmother tell him stories. He remembers her telling stories of her childhood in Europe. He loved to hear the folktales she told. "The best present I ever received was a volume of *Grimm's Fairy Tales,* which I loved so much that I literally read it to pieces," Kimmel recalls. The fairy tales and folktales he heard as a boy inspired him to retell these stories in his own books.

When Kimmel finished high school, he attended college to study to become an elementary school teacher. He graduated from college in 1967 and earned a Ph.D. in education in 1973. He worked as a university professor until 1994, when he quit teaching to devote all his time to writing.

> *"When I write a story, I read it aloud over and over again many times, trying to capture the music and rhythm of the words. So you might say that what I'm trying to do is capture in written words the experience of listening to the spoken word."*

KIMMEL'S FIRST BIG SUCCESS WAS HIS BOOK
HERSHEL AND THE HANUKKAH GOBLINS.

A Selected Bibliography of Kimmel's Work

The Frog Princess: A Tlingit Legend from Alaska (2006)

Horn for Louis (2005)

Cactus Soup (2004)

Wonders and Miracles: A Passover Companion (2003)

The Castle of Cats: A Story from Ukraine (2002)

The Jar of Fools: Eight Hanukkah Stories from Chelm (2000)

The Birds' Gift: A Ukrainian Easter Story (1999)

Sirko and the Wolf: A Ukrainian Tale (1997)

Billy Lazroe and the King of the Sea: A Tale of the Northwest (1996)

One Eye, Two Eyes, Three Eyes: A Hutzul Tale (1996)

Anansi and the Talking Melon (1994)

The Gingerbread Man (1993)

Boots and His Brothers: A Norwegian Tale (1992)

Bearhead: A Russian Folktale (1991)

Hershel and the Hanukkah Goblins (1989)

Anansi and the Moss-Covered Rock (1988)

The Tartar's Sword (1974)

Kimmel's first book, *The Tartar's Sword,* was published in 1974. Many of the stories Kimmell retells are stories he heard as child. He also finds material among the large collection of stories and folktales he has collected.

In his books, Kimmel emphasizes the telling of a story. "Stories aren't dead relics, preserved in a jar and put into a glass case for people to gawk at," Kimmel says. "They are alive, and like all living things they grow and change. You are not the same person you

"I love old things: old books, old pictures, old tools, old songs, and especially old stories."

were yesterday. You are not the person you will be tomorrow. So it is with stories. They change each time they are told."

Kimmel travels around the country as a storyteller. He is also known as an expert on children's literature. He lives with his family in Oregon where he continues to write books for children and young people.

❧

WHERE TO FIND OUT MORE ABOUT ERIC KIMMEL

BOOKS

McElmeel, Sharron L. *100 Most Popular Picture Book Authors and Illustrators: Biographical Sketches and Bibliographies.* Englewood, Colo.: Libraries Unlimited, 2000.

Silvey, Anita, ed. *The Essential Guide to Children's Books and Their Creators.* Boston: Houghton Mifflin Company, 2002.

WEB SITES

CHILDRENS LITERATURE
http://www.childrenslit.com/f_kimmel.html
To read biographical information about Eric Kimmel

ERIC A. KIMMEL HOME PAGE
http://www.ericakimmel.com/
For information about the author and his works

BESIDES WRITING, KIMMEL ENJOYS BIRD WATCHING, BAKING BREAD, SPINNING, RIDING HORSES, AND PLAYING THE BANJO.

Dick King-Smith

Born: March 27, 1922

Dick King-Smith did not begin his writing career until later in his life. He was fifty-six years old when his first children's book was published. He worked as a farmer, salesman, and teacher before becoming a writer. Since then, he has written more than eighty-five books for children and young people. His best-known books include *Babe: The Gallant Pig, The Invisible Dog, The Mouse Butcher,* and *Dragon Boy.*

Dick King-Smith was born on March 27, 1922, in Gloucestershire, England. As a child, Dick was interested in writing poetry. He had no interest in becoming a children's book author.

King-Smith attended college in the late 1930s. When he finished college, he

KING-SMITH'S BOOK *THE SHEEP-PIG* WAS PUBLISHED IN THE UNITED STATES AS *BABE: THE GALLANT PIG.* THE BOOK WAS ADAPTED INTO THE MOTION PICTURE *BABE* IN 1995. THE MOVIE WAS NOMINATED FOR SEVERAL ACADEMY AWARDS.

joined the British army. He fought in Europe during World War II and was wounded.

After he left the army, King-Smith and his wife moved to a farm near where he was born. King-Smith was a farmer for more than twenty years. He loved farming and loved the animals he raised on his farm. Though he worked hard, it was difficult to earn a living as a farmer. He needed to find another job. He worked for three years for a company that sold coats to firefighters. He also worked in a shoe factory. Then he decided to become a teacher.

King-Smith returned to college to be trained as a teacher. He became an

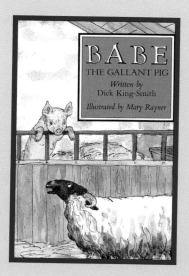

A Selected Bibliography of King-Smith's Work

Catlady (2006)
Golden Goose (2005)
Clever Lollipop (200 3)
Funny Frank (2002)
Billy the Bird (2001)
Mysterious Miss Slade (2000)
Charlie Muffin's Miracle Mouse (1999)
Mr. Ape (1998)
The Water Horse (1998)
A Mouse Called Wolf (1997)
The Stray (1996)
Harriet's Hare (1995)
Dragon Boy (1994)
The Invisible Dog (1993)
The Robber Boy (1991)
Ace, the Very Important Pig (1990)
Martin's Mice (1988)
Harry's Mad (1984)
Babe: The Gallant Pig (1983)
The Mouse Butcher (1982)
The Fox Busters (1978)

King-Smith's Major Literary Award

1985 Boston Globe-Horn Book Fiction Honor Book
Babe: The Gallant Pig

"*As for trying to fill a need in children's literature, if I am, it is to produce books that can afford adults some pleasure when they read to their children. I write for fun.*"

elementary school teacher when he was fifty-three years old. He worked as a teacher for seven years before retiring. While working as a teacher, King-Smith began thinking about writing books for children. His time as a teacher helped him understand what children like to read. His experience as a farmer was also important to him as a writer.

He began using his memories of being a farmer to write his books. He remembered how foxes sometimes came onto his farm and killed the chickens. He decided to write a book in which the chickens work together to chase away the foxes. His first book, *The Fox Busters,* was published in 1978. "I write about animals because I've always kept them, I'm interested

"*If there is a philosophical point behind what I write, I'm not especially conscious of it; maybe I do stress the need for courage, something we all wish we had more of, and I also do feel strongly for underdogs.*"

KING-SMITH DOES NOT USE A COMPUTER WHEN HE WRITES. HE WRITES HIS STORIES BY HAND AND THEN TYPES THEM ON HIS OLD TYPEWRITER.

in them, I know a bit about them, and I know that children like them," King-Smith notes. "Anyway, it's such fun putting words into their mouths."

King-Smith has written many children's books. Along with his writing, King-Smith has worked on children's television shows in England. He was involved in the shows *Tumbledown Farm* and *Rub-a-Dub-Tub.* King-Smith currently lives in England near the town where he was born.

❧

WHERE TO FIND OUT MORE ABOUT DICK KING-SMITH

BOOK

Silvey, Anita, ed. *The Essential Guide to Children's Books and Their Creators.* Boston: Houghton Mifflin Company, 2002.

WEB SITES

FANTASTIC FICTION
http://www.fantasticfiction.co.uk/k/dick-king-smith/
To read a biography and list of works

RANDOM HOUSE
http://www.randomhouse.com/kids/dickkingsmith/
For biographical information about Dick King-Smith

KING-SMITH LIVES WITH HIS WIFE IN A SMALL COTTAGE THAT WAS BUILT IN THE SEVENTEENTH CENTURY. HIS HOUSE IS MORE THAN **300** YEARS OLD.

Norma Klein

Born: May 13, 1938
Died: April 25, 1989

Norma Klein was known for writing stories for young people about realistic issues. She was not afraid to write about problems that young people may face. Her books deal with topics such as divorce, dating, sexuality, and racism. She also wrote books for adults. Her most popular books for young people include *Girls Can Be Anything; Love Is One of the Choices: A Novel; Sunshine: A Novel;* and *Mom, the Wolf Man, and Me.*

Norma Klein was born on May 13, 1938, in New York City. Growing up in the city, she always thought about being a writer. When

---

KLEIN TAUGHT COURSES IN FICTION AT YALE AND WESLEYAN UNIVERSITIES.

Klein finished high school, she attended Barnard College and Columbia University in New York City.

Klein began her career writing short stories and books for adults. In the 1960s and 1970s, she had many short stories published in literary magazines. She enjoyed writing short stories but found it difficult to get them published. She decided to focus instead

> *"I began writing children's books after reading the millionth picture book to my older daughter and figuring I would like to give it a try."*

on writing novels. In 1972, her first book was published. It included a novella and five of her short stories.

After the birth of her first daughter, Klein became interested in writing for young people. She started by writing picture books. Klein then decided to write books for older kids. She thought she would have an easier time publishing these books. Her first book for young people, *Mom, the Wolf Man, and Me,* was also published in 1972. The book was successful and inspired Klein to write other books for older kids.

While other authors write books for either boys or girls, Klein tried to write books that would be interesting for both. She used both boys and girls as main characters in her books. Klein was known for understanding the topics that interest young people. She sometimes wrote

---

Mom, the Wolf Man, and Me was made into a film in 1979.

GIRLS CAN BE ANYTHING

by NORMA KLEIN

illustrated by ROY DOTY

AB 17 $3.95

A Selected Bibliography of Klein's Work

Just Friends (1990)

Learning How to Fall (1989)

Going Backwards (1986)

Love Is One of the Choices: A Novel (1978)

Confessions of an Only Child (1974)

Sunshine: A Novel (1974)

Girls Can Be Anything (1973)

Mom, the Wolf Man, and Me (1972)

about issues that are meaningful to kids but upsetting to adults.

Many of Klein's books have been controversial. Several of her books have been targeted by groups wanting them removed from libraries. These groups do not believe the books are appropriate for young people. Klein did not want to cause trouble with her books. She wanted to write about what kids actually experience. "I'm not a rebel, trying to stir things up just to be provocative. I'm doing it because I feel like writing about real life," Klein noted.

Klein wrote more than forty books for young people. She also wrote more than sixty short stories for magazines.

> *"I found I enjoyed writing for children very much, partly perhaps because I got such a warm response to Mom."*

She published two or three books each year after she became a writer. Klein died on April 25, 1989. She was fifty years old.

WHERE TO FIND OUT MORE ABOUT NORMA KLEIN

BOOKS

Something about the Author. Autobiography Series.
Vol. 1. Detroit: Gale Research, 1986.

Sutherland, Zena. *Children and Books.*
New York: Addison Wesley Longman, 1997.

THE PEN/NORMA KLEIN AWARD HONORS KLEIN AND IS GIVEN FOR CHILDREN'S FICTION. IT IS SPONSORED BY KLEIN'S HUSBAND.

Suzy Kline

Born: August 27, 1943

It's no surprise that Suzy Kline knows what goes in on the classroom. She has been a second- and third-grade teacher for many years. Her classroom experiences have led Suzy to create such memorable children's book characters as Herbie Jones, Horrible Harry, and Mary Marony.

Suzy Weaver was born in Berkeley, California, on August 27, 1943. Her father worked in real estate and her mother was a housewife. After finishing high school, Weaver went to Columbia University in New York City for a year. Then she transferred to the University

KLINE STARTED WRITING WHEN SHE WAS EIGHT YEARS OLD. HER FIRST WRITING EFFORTS WERE LETTERS TO HER GRANDFATHER, WHO LIVED IN INDIANA. IN THOSE LETTERS, KLINE DESCRIBED WHAT WAS HAPPENING IN HER LIFE.

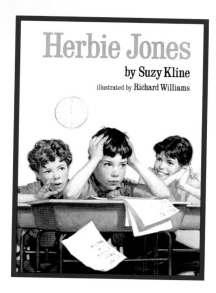

Herbie Jones
by Suzy Kline
illustrated by Richard Williams

A Selected Bibliography of Kline's Work

Horrible Harry and the Triple Revenge (2006)

Horrible Harry and the Goog (2005)

Horrible Harry and the Locked Closet (2004)

Horrible Harry and the Dragon War (2002)

Horrible Harry Goes to the Moon (2000)

Marvin and the Meanest Girl (2000)

Molly's in a Mess (1999)

Song Lee and the "I Hate You" Notes (1999)

Horrible Harry Moves Up to Third Grade (1998)

Horrible Harry and the Purple People (1997)

Marvin and the Mean Words (1997)

Horrible Harry and the Dungeon (1996)

Mary Marony and the Chocolate Surprise (1995)

Song Lee and the Leech Man (1995)

Mary Marony, Mummy Girl (1994)

Song Lee and the Hamster Hunt (1994)

Herbie Jones and the Birthday Showdown (1993)

Song Lee in Room 2B (1993)

Herbie Jones and the Dark Attic (1992)

Horrible Harry and the Kickball Wedding (1992)

Orp Goes to the Hoop (1991)

Horrible Harry's Secret (1990)

Orp and the Chop Suey Burgers (1990)

Herbie Jones and Hamburger Head (1989)

Horrible Harry and the Green Slime (1989)

ORP (1989)

Herbie Jones and the Monster Ball (1988)

Ooops! (1988)

Herbie Jones and the Class Gift (1987)

What's the Matter with Herbie Jones? (1986)

Don't Touch (1985)

Herbie Jones (1985)

SHHHH! (1984)

of California at Berkeley. After she graduated from Berkeley, she attended California State College in Hayward to get her teaching credentials. Her first job was in an elementary school in Richmond, California.

While she was working in Richmond, Weaver married Rufus O. Kline. Her husband was also a teacher and writer, although he taught college students rather than little kids.

> *"Being a teacher is the most difficult job in the world. At least twice a week I feel like going to an island and not returning to the classroom. But the truth is, I wouldn't do anything else."*

The Klines became the parents of two daughters, Jennifer and Emily.

In 1976, the Kline family moved to Connecticut. That's where Kline began writing books for children. Her first books were picture books for young children. *SHHHH!* was published in 1984. This book describes a little girl who is told to be quiet by many people during the day. In the end, she finds an acceptable way to be loud. *Don't Touch* was published in 1985. It shows a little boy who is scolded for touching dangerous things until he finds some modeling clay, which he can play with and touch all he wants.

In 1985, Kline published her first book for elementary school students, which introduced a little boy named Herbie Jones to the world of children's books. The books about Herbie show an ordinary little boy and the challenges and delights he faces every day at home and at school. In *What's the Matter with Herbie Jones?* for example, Herbie must contend with a spelling bee, a school dance, and a girlfriend he doesn't want!

Later, Kline added more "regular kids" to her stories, including a mischievous troublemaker known as Horrible Harry, a little girl who

WHEN KLINE VISITS SCHOOLS, SHE ALWAYS BRINGS A BOX OF REJECTION LETTERS AND UNPUBLISHED STORIES. SHE WANTS CHILDREN TO KNOW THAT NOT EVERYTHING SHE WRITES IS GOOD ENOUGH TO BE PUBLISHED.

stutters named Mary Marony, bully Marvin Higgins, shy Song Lee, and Orville Rudemeyer Pygenski Jr., who hates his name and prefers to be called Orp.

> *"Everyday life is full of stories if we just take the time to write them."*

Along with writing about children and teaching them, Kline enjoys visiting schools and talking about her books and characters. For Kline, nothing is more fun than surrounding herself with kids—both real and imaginary!

❧

WHERE TO FIND OUT MORE ABOUT SUZY KLINE

BOOK

McElmeel, Sharron L. *100 Most Popular Children's Authors: Biographical Sketches and Bibliographies..* Englewood, Colo.: Libraries Unlimited, 1999.

WEB SITES

EDUCATIONAL PAPERBACK SOCIETY
http://www.edupaperback.org/showauth.cfm?authid=241
For biographical information about Suzy Klein

SUZY KLINE HOME PAGE
http://www.suzykline.com/
For a biographical sketch of Suzy Kline, information about her books, and interactive read-aloud excerpts from some of her works

KLINE HAS WRITTEN AND DIRECTED SCHOOL PLAYS.

INDEX

H

Haddix, Margaret Peterson, 4: 12–15
Hamilton, Virginia, 1: 19, 21; 4: 16–19
Handler, Daniel. *See* Snicket, Lemony.
Hansen, Joyce, 4: 20–23
Haskins, James, 4: 24–27
Hay, Timothy. *See* Brown, Margaret Wise.
Henkes, Kevin, 4: 28–31
Henry, Marguerite, 4: 32–35
Hesse, Karen, 4: 36–39
Hiaasen, Carl, 4: 40–43
Hill, Eric, 4: 44–47
Hinton, S. E., 4: 48–51
Hispanic American authors and illustrators. *See also* African American authors and illustrators; Asian American authors and illustrators; British authors and illustrators; Native American authors and illustrators.
    Aruego, José, 1: 50–53
    Garza, Carmen Lomas, 3: 120–123
    Ryan, Pam Muñoz, 7: 40–43, 78, 79
Historical fiction. *See also* Biographies; Fiction; Folktales.
    Avi, 1: 54–57; 8: 90, 137
    Collier, Christopher, 2: 84–87
    Collier, James Lincoln, 2: 84–87
    Curtis, Christopher Paul, 2: 116–119
    Cushman, Karen, 2: 120–124
    Dorris, Michael, 3: 12–15
    Fleischman, Paul, 3: 68–71
    Forbes, Esther, 3: 80–83
    Fox, Paula, 3: 88–91
    Fritz, Jean, 3: 100–103; 8: 134
    Goble, Paul, 3: 144–147
    Hamilton, Virginia, 1: 19, 21; 4: 16–19
    Hansen, Joyce, 4: 20–23
    Hesse, Karen, 4: 36–39
    Hopkinson, Deborah, 4: 68–71
    Konigsburg, E. L., 5: 8–11
    Lasky, Kathryn, 5: 16–19
    Lawson, Robert, 5: 24–27
    Lenski, Lois, 2: 9, 10, 11; 5: 44–47
    Lowry, Lois, 5: 88–91
    McCully, Emily Arnold, 5: 124–127
    McKissack, Patricia, 5: 140–143
    O'Dell, Scott, 6: 56–59
    Osborne, Mary Pope, 6: 60–63
    Paterson, Katherine, 6: 84–87

    Ringgold, Faith, 7: 16–19
    Sobol, Donald, 7: 124–127
    Speare, Elizabeth George, 7: 132–135
    St. George, Judith, 8: 16–19
    Wilder, Laura Ingalls, 8: 88–91
    Yep, Laurence, 8: 124–127
Historical nonfiction. *See also* Biographies; Nonfiction.
    Blumberg, Rhoda, 1: 98–101
    Brandenberg, Aliki, 1: 114–117
    Bulla, Clyde Robert, 2: 8–11
    Collier, Christopher, 2: 84–87
    Collier, James Lincoln, 2: 84–87
    Cooney, Barbara, 2: 88–91
    Freedman, Russell, 3: 92–95
    Giblin, James Cross, 3: 136–139
    Hansen, Joyce, 4: 20–23
    Haskins, James, 4: 24–27
    Lester, Julius, 5: 48–51
    Patent, Dorothy Hinshaw, 6: 80–83
    Provensen, Alice, 6: 144–147
    Provensen, Martin, 6: 144–147
    Ringgold, Faith, 7: 16–19
    Speare, Elizabeth George, 7: 132–135
    Stanley, Diane, 7: 144–147
    St. George, Judith, 8: 16–19
    Yolen, Jane, 2: 142; 8: 82, 128–131, 134
Hoban, Tana, 4: 52–55
Hoff, Syd, 4: 56–59
Hogrogian, Nonny, 4: 60–63
Hopkins, Lee Bennett, 4: 64–67
Hopkinson, Deborah, 4: 68–71
Horror. *See also* Fantasy; Fiction; Mysteries; Science fiction.
    Bellairs, John, 1: 82–85
    Philbrick, Rodman, 6: 100–103
    Ren Wright, Betty, 7: 12–15
    Stine, R. L., 8: 20–23
Horvath, Polly, 4: 72–75
Howe, James, 4: 76–79
Hughes, Langston, 1: 156; 4: 80–83; 5: 147
Hurwitz, Johanna, 4: 84–87
Hutchins, Pat, 4: 88–91
Hyman, Trina Schart, 4: 92–95

I

Illustrators. *See also* Picture books.
    Ahlberg, Janet, 1: 22–25